Images of Salvation

in the fiction of

C. S. Lewis

by Clyde S. Kilby

Harold Shaw Publishers
Wheaton, Illinois

cover illustration: Tim Kirk

Copyright © 1978
by Harold Shaw Publishers.
All rights reserved.
No part of this book
may be reproduced in any form
without written permission
from the publisher.

ibrary of Congress Catalog Card Number 78-53011
ISBN 0-87788-391-2

First printing, October, 1978

Printed in the United States of America

To Jean & Kenneth Hansen

Introduction

When I first discovered C. S. Lewis, and for many years after-wards, I neglected his fiction in favor of his expository works. It was not because I was a disbeliever in fiction, for I was by profession a teacher of literature. I knew that a novel or play or poem might convey great and permanent meanings into one's life. But in those early years of reading Lewis I was overwhelmed by the powerful logic of works such as Mere Christianity, Miracles and The Problem of Pain. I felt that no Christian I had ever read, unless it were G. K. Chesterton, had spoken so clearly or so cogently for Christianity. I belonged, as I still do, among conservative Christians, and in those days, when liberal theology seemed to be taking over the religious world, we were all seeking explicitly lucid and logical statements in defense of our faith. Lewis became our hero—at least he became mine.

It was long after I had discovered Lewis that I began to turn with enthusiasm to his creative writings. While recognizing its adroit-ness, I had felt something less than the common enthusiasm for The Screwtape Letters, but his other fiction of the 1940's and early 1950's looked better and better to me the more I read of it. Like so many others, I gobbled up the Narnia stories, recognizing that they belonged among the classics for children and were an equally golden gift for adults. Without downgrading the significance of Lewis's expository writings, I came to believe an even greater potential lay in the stories he produced.

The time came when, invited to teach college courses in Lewis, I had to make a choice. I chose the fiction. And now, after many years of living in the Lewis landscape, there is no doubt left in my mind. In both sorts of his writing great meaning is presented with unusual skill and strength. Yet I find (among young people in particular) that a genuinely successful story is likely to make a deeper, more lasting impact than a theoretical presentation of prin-ciples. A splendidly created character or set of circumstances, by *drawing us into its own world, allows us not simply to evaluate but actually to experience, to stand in the very shoes of hero or villain. Professor Tolkien has well said that we create by the very laws by which we are made, meaning that fiction, when done well, is as intricate or mysterious as life itself.*

C. S. Lewis was himself a teacher of literature and a literary critic of note. He knew that a good piece of creative writing does not come easily, and the records show that from early childhood he wished to be a writer and especially a creative one. He wrote much as a boy, work not really good but by its very quantity adequate to show a will to write and a considerable knowledge of how effectual writing takes place. And it is clear that his apprenticeship paid off. When Lewis died in 1963 he left twenty-three Christian works, all of which remain in print today and are being read by literally millions of people. Of these, fourteen were works of creative fiction. It is with these fourteen that the present book is concerned.

This is not a book about Lewis's theology. Rather it is related to his creative use of images, symbols and illustrations in his presentation of Biblical truths and the Christian way of life. Let it be said that nowhere in this book is the word "image" used in the sense of a trick but rather as a means of presenting what cannot be portrayed as clearly in an expository fashion. In Les Miserables *Victor Hugo describes a good bishop who, for the edification of his people in one parish, would relate particular instances of the outcome of either goodness or immorality in another parish and who, if no specific illustration of that kind came to mind, would "invent parables, going straight to his object, with images, which was the very eloquence of Jesus Christ, convincing and persuasive." Our Lord was indeed an habitual teller of tales. Here, in C. S. Lewis, we find the particular cases of Jane and Mark Studdock, Uncle Andrew, Devine, the Dimbles, Wormwood, Puddleglum, Prince Caspian, Orual and dozens of others who sought the pearl of great price, or else rejected it, and such and such were the results.*

As for theology as a branch of learning, Lewis, without in the least eschewing it, left its dogmatic presentation to professional theologians. He was more concerned with the use of theology than with its systematic expression. The theology is there, as it must always be, underlying the landscape, rockribbed as mountains, but Lewis was wise enough to lay claim to being no more than what he actually was, a layman writing to laymen about "mere" Christianity. One feels, with immense gratitude, how deliberately wise he was to remain as far as possible outside divisionary realms, to strive with all his wisdom to stand on the great Christian creeds —the ground that is regarded as orthodox Christianity—and to avoid association with any "camp" other than the clearly Biblical one.

My primary purpose in this book is to be useful to those who are in the process of discovering C. S. Lewis; who have, indeed, read these tales at least once. Charles and Mary Lamb did English literature a great service in their re-telling of Shakespeare's Tales. In the same style I have tried, first, to remind my readers of the outline of Lewis's stories by re-telling them as simply and meaningfully as I can, and then noting, with as little piousness and pretentiousness as possible, the Christian involvements of each story.

Thus each chapter in this volume consists of two sections: first, a summary of the Lewis story or stories under discussion and then a section in which parallels are drawn between this story and the life and belief of the Christian. I have used the term "image" in its broadest sense—that of a concept or idea whose meaning carries over from one context to another. I am fully aware that there are many more meanings in any one of his stories than I have identified. My hope is that by showing some examples of Christian analogy I may encourage the reader to go on and recognize more on his own. I know of one manuscript on the meaning of Till We Have Faces *that is as long as the novel itself. Similar research could probably be done with any story Lewis wrote, but obviously that cannot be my intention here.*

I should warn you that Lewis is an author whose writing changes people. Unless you are prepared to undergo change, do not read his books. He is not simply another writer with a "point of view." His subtleties of plot and character, his literary devices, for he has plenty of them, are not used from a desire to appear clever, or shocking, but that his reader may have a wider view of the laws and the love of the Lord God. Yet he greatly disliked the notion of telling a story as the sugarcoating for a sermon and never forgot that a story must be, in itself, both convincing and enjoyable, for only in a good story may the reader himself become a participant.

I acknowledge with deep gratitude the enthusiastic editorial assistance of Luci Shaw. I am also grateful to Thomas Wilson Burrows for his translation and explanation of a number of foreign words and phrases and classical allusions in The Pilgrim's Regress.

Let me again remind the reader of my assumption throughout that he has first read the particular books by Lewis which I here discuss.

Because Lewis's books have been published in different editions, with varied pagination, any references in this volume are to chapters and sections only.

Unless otherwise indicated, all Biblical references are to the King James Version.

My thanks are due to the Macmillan Company, Harcourt, Brace, Jovanovich, and Wm. B. Eerdmans for the use of quotations.

I
The Eve
Who Did Not Fall

Out of the Silent Planet
Perelandra

Out of the Silent Planet
Taking a lengthy walk through English countryside, Elwin Ransom, having been refused a place at the inn where he expected to stay overnight and thus being forced to go forward in the dark, accidentally fell into the hands of Weston, the physicist, and Devine, the lover of gold and what it brings of worldly pleasure. He was knocked on the head and shoved aboard their space ship bound for Malacandra (Mars). Despite his fears of awakening in space and his even greater apprehension at overhearing a plan by which he was to be handed over to the "natives" of Malacandra, Ransom experienced a hitherto unimaginable joy. He had always supposed space to be simply black and dead but now he found it filled with a sublime radiance. He watched, fascinated, as his own world receded and viewed with shining eyes and tingling blood glories he had never dreamed of. The majesty of stars and constellations, now seen from outside the contaminated atmosphere of earth, stabbed him with their brilliance and color. He kept thinking how the old word "heavens" was so much more appropriate and descriptive than the new word "space."

After a long flight and difficult landing on Malacandra, Ransom managed his escape. When he had run a long way and felt safe he began to look at this strange planet where everything seemed to leap skyward, even its purple vegetation rising brilliantly higher than trees on earth. He spent his first night beside a warm spring flowing down a little valley. Next day he came upon great yellow, furry beasts somewhat like giraffes. But his astonishment was boundless when he discovered another creature "something like a penguin, something like an otter, something like a seal," and found it could talk. Since Ransom was a philologist, his fear was overcome by the exciting possibility of learning the creature's language. He soon found that it was a *hross* whose name was Hyoi, and, not without some hesitation, he allowed it to take him on a long boat ride to its people. Welcomed by them, he began to acquire their language and also learned the manner of life of these extraordinary but intelligent beings. Their lives followed a simple agricultural pattern and they were great lovers of music and poetry. They also questioned him about his own world and were shocked to learn of its evils, for they were themselves innocent, being ruled by Oyarsa, a planetary angel under the authority of Maleldil (Christ).

Their only planetary enemy was the *hnakra* and though he sometimes killed a *hross* in their battles his presence added the sting of excitement to their existence. One day, while on a hunt for the *hnakra* they were seen from ambush by Weston and Devine who shot and killed Ransom's friend Hyoi, a deed which again reminded Ransom of the great contrast between this world and his own.

Ransom was ordered to go up a very high mountain and meet Augray, the shepherd *sorn*, grotesquely tall and spidery in body and movement and yet often more knowledgeable and logical than Ransom himself, and as devoted as the *hrossa* to Oyarsa and Maleldil. One thing Augray did was show Ransom, through a sort of telescope, his own world shining, very small but bright, in the black sky. As he again remembered the contrast between his fallen world and undefiled Malacandra, he felt deeply depressed.

After a time Augray took Ransom down the mountain to Meldilorn where he met the third sort of inhabitant of Malacandra, a creature rather like a frog or a grasshopper called a *pfifltrigg*, one skilled in portraying character and the role of history by means of sculpture and painting. On Meldilorn Ransom was awed as he was led down a monolithic avenue filled with Malacandrian creatures and thousands, perhaps millions, of nearly invisible *eldils* filling earth and sky as they all silently awaited the appearance of their wise and loving Oyarsa. It was there that Ransom learned from Oyarsa the shocking fact that Earth had long before been estranged from the rest of the universe because a "bent" *eldil* (Satan) had caused its downfall.

There also Weston and Devine were placed on trial and the arrogant foolishness of Weston displayed. It was only through pity of their sad condition that the Oyarsa did not destroy the two. As for Ransom, he was offered the privilege of remaining on Malacandra or returning with Weston and Devine to Earth. Loving Malacandra, Random nevertheless felt the tug of his native soil and so entered the space ship and at last reached the place from which they had started, remembering Oyarsa's assurance that they should probably meet again and also his warning to keep his eyes open to the prevention of further evils on the part of Weston and Devine.

Perelandra

After a time Ransom readied himself for a second voyage into the heavens, this time to Perelandra (Venus) and not by space ship but by the summons of the Oyarsa himself, for he had discovered with amazement and joy that his first trip was not accidental but devised in order that he should become the agent of beings who made their habitation in no one planet but ranged the breadth of the celestial heavens. Not knowing what he should find on Perelandra or what assignments he might be required to perform, nevertheless he prepared to go, willing to place full confidence in the Oyarsa. Actually he had found that the Oyarsa, and indeed all planetary angels, owed allegiance to Maleldil (Christ), the "shining sent one."

So in the grey chill of an early morning Ransom and his friend carried a prepared "casket" out of the house, the friend both terrified and unbelieving as he heard Ransom's good-bye and saw him lie down in this unique conveyance. With trembling fingers he followed Ransom's instructions to fasten the lid. A moment later the vehicle was gone, he knew not how, and he returned home convinced he would never see Ransom again.

More than a year later Ransom returned. Appearing to be in perfect health and greatly younger, he told the story of his visit. He had landed in water, for Perelandra was more fluid than terrestrial, and his casket had dissolved. A good swimmer, he had looked about him at a "landscape" of unimaginable glory and tingling reality. He found a floating island and crawled onto it. Above him he saw a golden sky and about him a forest of unearthly trees yielding undreamed of fragrances and fruits which satisfied him better than the finest of Earth had ever done. At night he slept in a warm darkness perfect for repose while his island moved gently with the movement of the waves.

Here was a man from fallen Earth who was personally conducted by Maleldil first to Malacandra, a planet where war had once been experienced but where the inhabitants lived in continual quietness of spirit and peace with each other, knowing death but not fear and obeying without question its planetary Oyarsa, himself the agent of Maleldil. Now, on this second voyage, he found himself in a totally unfallen planet where death was unknown and a king and queen made in the very image of Maleldil had been appointed to people the planet, living always in utter innocence and warm and immediate relationship with him as well as with sky, earth and water. Though Maleldil was not bodily present he was nevertheless as eternally with them as the constant murmur of the waters bearing up their glorious floating islands.

But why had the Oyarsa sent Ransom to Perelandra? Was

it simply that he might feel there the overflowing ecstasy on every hand and discover everything good in himself reaching out in joyful acceptance? Was he there only to see the perfections of Perelandra accentuated by his recollections of the lesser and corrupted things of Earth? He remembered that his journey to Malacandra was by no means accidental and he wondered what motive other than pure enjoyment had brought him to this planet of love.

Looking about him he concluded he was the sole human inhabitant of this glorious country. One day to his surprise and delight, he saw another being on another island floating nearby—a woman beautiful as a goddess. They met with mutual astonishment, as she was looking for her husband and at first thought Ransom was he. The first discovery Ransom made was that he could speak easily with her in the language of Malacandra. Indeed he found that all the universe had a common language except for his own planet Earth. He had already (on Malacandra) become much ashamed of his own "bent" world with its wars, its prostitution and its ubiquitous selfishness, and now, as he looked about him and talked with the Lady he was overwhelmed by the truth of what men on Earth called "The Fall." For the first time in his life Ransom now saw an *unfallen* world of pristine beauty and unpretentious goodness. Indeed the Lady, surrounded by a multitude of beasts, birds and fish which made it evident that they looked upon her as their queen, began to ask Ransom questions which shook him into vast new realizations. Ransom told her he had come to Perelandra in peace. "What is peace?" she asked. Peace? To be ignorant of peace, not so much from its absence as from its unending presence—could one have so complete a peace as not to realize its existence? Ransom was sharply reminded of the fragility of earthly peace, how quickly it came and went no matter how earnestly it was desired.

Ransom naturally sought to learn about the Lady's husband and people. He asked her about her home. "What is home?" she inquired. He learned that wherever Maleldil was seemed home to her. As she spoke of Maleldil Ransom, already overcome by the bliss of his surroundings, felt a mysterious pressure on his shoulders as the air around him seemed to intensify, making his legs weak and causing him to sink down. Had there been a time like this in the history of his own world when Maleldil was immediately present and easily communicated with? Had there been a time when all creation was a perfect unity of love and unexpressed, yet perfectly felt, relationship?

Ransom discovered that the only two human inhabitants of Perelandra were this Lady and her husband, the King. The Lady asked about Ransom's mother and learned she was dead. "What is death?" the Lady interrogated. Ransom had to reply that death is so loathsome and foul smelling that Maleldil himself had wept over it. But why, asked the Lady, looking at the moving water under their island, should not we be glad for every wave which Maleldil rolls towards us? For the first time she was beginning to understand the possibility of choice, that she might want something other than Maleldil's wave. Hitherto she had known only perfect oneness with Maleldil, and now it dawned on her that she was herself, a separate entity, and therefore able to choose. "I thought that I was carried in the will of Him I love, but now I see that I walk with it," she said. Now Ransom began to see how easily choosing for oneself, though not an evil thing, might lead to evil, and he explained as best he could the perils inherent in choice.

The next day, as they continued to speak with one another, they heard a sound far away. It signalled the arrival of Weston, the scientist who had long before knocked Ransom on the head and taken him by space ship to Malacandra. Now he was visiting Perelandra, and for no better motive. Like all men everywhere, fearing and hating coffins and the palor of death and decay, he had wished to spread our race from one planet to another until such time as the human superman would flourish godlike in all the universe. Now his intention was to spread "spirituality." When Ransom insisted that there are evil spirits as well as good ones, Weston disagreed violently. *"Your* Devil and *your* God," he told Ransom, "are both pictures of the same Force." Ransom learned that Weston had been taught the language of Perelandra by bent eldils on earth, and Weston made it clear that he was in process of becoming an incarnation of the world Life-Force, as he called it. Finally Weston, in a moment of egotistical drama, called upon this Force to take possession of him. He was instantly spun round as if hit by a bullet and, momentarily unconscious, fell to the ground. Thus he became the Un-man who would henceforth be the agent of Satan himself, who by an ancient decree of Maleldil could not depart from the vicinity of Earth.

From now on Weston the Un-man began to approach the Lady and, using a subtlety made all the more devilish by the fact that all his arguments stemmed from subjects already discussed in her innocent conversations with Ransom, began his strategy of seduction. The Lady and her husband had been told by Maleldil that, simply as an indication of their willing obedience to him, they were not to remain overnight on a small portion of fixed land on Perelandra. You have learned from Ransom, said the Un-man to her, that you have more than one way in which to walk. Now do you not see, said he, that Ransom and I have been sent all the way to Perelandra by Maleldil to open your eyes to new and wonderful things? Maleldil wants you to be a "full woman," not like your beasts and your fish who do only what they are told. Women on Earth, he explained, reach out for new kinds of good and pass them along to their husbands and their husbands love them for it.

Now Ransom began to see why he had been sent by Maleldil to Perelandra. The continued perfection of that planet was threatened and he, Elwin Ransom, an ordinary man, was there to do all in his power to save it. He was the agent of Maleldil as the Un-man was the agent of Earth's bent Oyarsa, Satan. He was to wrestle not against human flesh and blood (as he had supposed) but against spiritual wickedness of cosmic subtlety. Ransom found the Un-man's dialog with the Lady continued both in darkness and daylight, always with great intensity and seeming logic. The main appeal was to the Lady's selfhood. Did not Maleldil intend, by sending Ransom and him to Perelandra, to bring good news to her, the news that she was really "her own"? Having done this wonderful thing, he now wanted from her a sign that she accepted this news. And how could she better demonstrate to Maleldil her awareness of such news than by the simple act of deliberately choosing her own way, by disobeying him? Remember, said he, the Fixed Land where Maleldil had told her not to stay overnight? She must go there and remain and thus assure him of her new awareness of selfhood. Ransom wanted her to remain "young" always and never grow to maturity, but if she chose the way of courage, said Weston, he would teach her many things, especially Death.

Of course Ransom constantly urged the Lady not to believe the Un-man, but it seemed to him that his own arguments were weak and the Lady was slowly being won over. In desperation Ransom finally told her the story of another Eden and how one like the Un-man persuaded Adam and Eve to do the forbidden thing. As he described the vast evil that came of it, the Un-man vigorously insisted that instead much good came of it, greatest of all that Maleldil himself became a man. Ransom was stunned by this perverted reasoning. He told the Lady that though good did indeed come of it (for Maleldil can always bring good out of evil) yet the choice made by Adam and Eve was not itself good. Ransom then turned to the Un-man and asked whether *he* rejoiced in Maleldil's becoming a man, to which he could only open his mouth and howl like a melancholy dog.

The battle continued for days. When the Un-man failed in factual argument, an occurrence for which Ransom gave all credit to the presence of Maleldil, he turned to another sort of temptation. He began an appeal to the Lady's emotions and endeavored to persuade her to become a creative heroine, famed now or else acknowledged after death for her accomplishments. He told her innumerable stories of great deeds and great risks, all directed toward making her think of herself as an instructor to her own husband in many new ideas. Self-sacrifice he recommended to her as a role for her future—tragic self-sacrifice. Let her be a martyr for everybody to admire. In all of his suggestions there was a veiled appeal to egotism. Let her become her own person, as man had done on Earth.

Ransom, of course, watched intently for any change in the Lady's attitude. One problem was that both Ransom and the Lady needed sleep while the Un-man did not. His nefarious devices never ceased. Ransom awoke one morning to find the Un-man and the Lady robed in purple and blue feathers torn by him from the birds of Perelandra as well as chaplets of silver leaves on their heads. The scene was climaxed by the Un-man's fishing out of his luggage a small mirror and handing it to the Lady. Never having seen a mirror she had to be instructed as to how to see herself in it. Once she did, a new expression came into her face and some of her own mysterious beauty went out of it. What she experienced for the first time was fear, for she now saw fully her separate self and was afraid of it. But the Un-man promptly proposed that she accept fear and taste it on behalf of her husband and future generations. He also tried to persuade her to hold onto the mirror, and thus acquire something to her personal advantage that others would not have. The Un-man had clothed her and caused her to see her own beauty only that she might elevate and dramatize her self.

Now it appeared that by dint of sheer pressure the Lady

would succumb. Thinking thus, Ransom began to ask himself why he alone must be expected to vanquish the very power of hell. The great Enemy was there. Why was not Maleldil also there? Such thoughts had hardly ceased when Ransom felt the darkness around him alive with such intensity that he knew Maleldil to be present. Indeed, Ransom now saw clearly that Maleldil had never been absent. As surely as the Enemy had sent the Un-man to Perelandra, Ransom saw that he also had been chosen and sent. Then a horrific idea dawned on him. He, he and no other, was responsible for the fate of Perelandra. This indeed, he realized, was the way all things were designed. "Either something or nothing must depend on individual choices." What would Elwin Ransom do? He had always thought of opposition to Satan as simply a "spiritual" affair. But by no rationalization could he avoid the simple fact that he was there, under the authority of Maleldil, to destroy the Enemy. Ransom remembered that he was an ordinary, middle-aged, balding man whose only physical struggles had been boyhood ones. He visualized the long, metallic fingernails of the Un-man and could imagine them ripping off strips of his flesh and simply pulling him apart until the life went out of him.

Now desperate, but clear about his duty, Ransom sought out the Un-man. He found him tearing to pieces one of a number of strangled birds whose blood was spattered over his chest. Ransom attacked and a bloody battle ensued. It turned out to be a contest between Ransom's blows to the Un-man's body and the Un-man's tearing nails. Realizing that what he fought was not merely a human of corrupted will but rather corruption itself, he fought with a true hatred of that corruption. Eventually he felt the Un-man's ribs crack and its jaw-bone break. It ran away. The chase led to the water and eventually to the death of the Un-man, but not before he had badly bitten Ransom's foot, a wound which was never to heal until he should again be carried back into the heavens, this time by the triumphant eldils.

Ransom, half dead himself, was a long time recovering. When he was finally well again he found himself present at a ceremony of unparalleled glory on a mountaintop where the Oyeresu of Malacandra and Perelandra brought the King and his Queen before all the creatures of the planet and there reaffirmed their everlasting loyalty to Maleldil and consciously assumed the lasting headship of the planet of Love.

After the ceremony Ransom was returned to Earth in his prepared casket. Some of the rose-red lilies from the mountaintop were put in with him before they bade him goodbye. But before his parting all and each had spoken their warm praise of Maleldil and the joyous fact that because of Ransom's faithfulness this planet would forever be free from the dread contagion which Earth must suffer until its great restoration.

(The third volume in the space trilogy, *That Hideous Strength*, will be discussed in chapter 6, "How to Get a Face Two Ways.")

∞

Out of the Silent Planet

Lewis constantly and consistently seeks to make us conscious of something we are forever neglecting, that is, man's true place in a universe endlessly overseen and directed by a God of love and of justice.

1. When Ransom packed his knapsack and began the pleasant holiday walk that would lead him first to Malacandra and later to Perelandra, he had no idea that God was carefully planting his footsteps. Nor did he know that God was instrumental in his being refused a room at the inn or in the interference of the weeping woman; least of all in his being knocked on the head. Neither would the reader ordinarily see God at work in these circumstances did not Lewis later explicitly identify them as part of the sovereign purpose of Maleldil. Thinking such facts over, one begins

to wonder whether initially Maleldil, intending Ransom to take this very walk, was not in his love of walking and in his father's encouragement long years before of the love of walking in his son, and so on backwards through events all the way to eternity past. "You saw me before I was born and scheduled each day of life before I began to breathe," says Psalm 139:16 (*The Living Bible*).

Equally under the sovereignty of God were Weston and Devine and their evil intention to carry off Ransom as a hostage, as they supposed, to the "natives" of Malacandra. They were totally unaware that Maleldil's agents stood unseen all about their space ship when it landed on Malacandra (XVIII).[1] Indeed, Ransom did not understand until long afterwards that the *hnakra* was made to appear when it did so that he might have opportunity to escape his captors.

2. The centrality of God as creator and sustainer of all the universe is likewise apparent. The *hrossa* were shocked when Ransom asked if Oyarsa, the planetary angel of Malacandra, had made the world. No, they quickly shouted, it was Maleldil the Young (Christ) who "made and still ruled" as he always had (VI). On the journey of the space ship home Ransom, now at last beginning to perceive and understand the true hierarchy of the universe, felt the "unseen presences" inside the space ship and hence felt small and frail "against a background of such immeasurable fullness" (XXI).

The idea of great supervising angels such as the Oyeresu is not unbiblical. According to Daniel 12:1, Michael is "the great prince in charge of the Jews."

3. Another image seen in many places in Lewis's fiction relates to the Fall of Man. Perhaps nowhere does he set it forth more clearly than in the contrasts between the unfallen heavens, the true and eternally glorious residence

---

[1]Here and throughout this volume Roman numerals refer to chapter numbers in the Lewis book under discussion.

of *eldils* (angels) and fallen Earth. Ransom had always thought of planets as places of true substance floating in the black void of space, but now he had to reverse his imagery. The heavens are "full of life" (XXI) while all planets, as such, are "waste spaces," mere "holes or gaps in the living heavens," with atmosphere thick and oppressive (VI). Even the planet Perelandra, though unfallen, contrasts with the true heavens in which it moves. We are told in Psalm 19:1 that the heavens declare not simply glory but *the glory of God*. Ransom, traveling in the true heavens, had a transcendent experience. And of course Lewis hopes his reader may also begin to open his eyes to the true glory of those same heavens. One may profitably ask himself when he has ever had, or even desired to have, such an experience.

The planet Earth and its human inhabitants are contrasted very explicitly with Malacandra and Perelandra, for Earth is a "bent" place (Lewis's striking metaphor for sin) which has a bent Oyarsa (Satan) and bent *eldils* who take significant part in Earth's affairs.

As part of this imagery we must also note that Lewis is indeed a believer in angels. Though angels are mentioned often in the Bible, Christians are slow to honor them with reality. Ransom himself was at first unable to see *eldils* and might never have discovered their existence had he not met someone who could see them. He learned that they come from Oyarsa, are hard to see unless one is "looking in the right place and at the right time," and may be mistaken for mere sunbeams or rustling leaves (XII); also that they are full of light rather than blood and travel as fast as light (XV). When Ransom actually heard the voice of an *eldil* he could no longer doubt its existence (XIII).

The Malacandrians found it almost impossible to understand Ransom's report of war, prostitution and other evils on earth (XIII, XVI), their own society being innocent of such "bent" behavior.

Lewis even takes advantage of the lighter mass of Mars

to allow for a "theme of perpendicularity" there (VIII), as if those who live on that planet experience God more easily and naturally. Thus the Malacandrians viewed humans as squat, crude, awkward and quite ignorant (XIX). We learn, to our surprise, that Malacandra might long ago have had space ships had they thought them desirable.

It was sin which caused Earth to become the silent planet, a place excluded by Maleldil from participation in the pure heavens. In later books we learn of a vast struggle between Maleldil and his greatest enemy and how finally that enemy was confined to a quarantine area beginning at Earth and extending to the moon (*That Hideous Strength*, XVI, 4). Indeed, Malacandra is also silent in its uppermost reaches, having suffered in millennia past when involved in the great struggle during which Satan brought "the cold death" to that land. Oyarsa had saved the rest of the planet by opening up warm springs (XVIII).

4. The word "Maleldil" troubles some readers who recall that the Latin prefix "mal" means bad or evil. The prefix here is from the Hebrew "Malac" meaning "one sent from God." (Cp. the prophet Malachi in the Bible.)

5. Always Lewis reiterates the need for direct and unfailing obedience to God. In this story it is illustrated by Ransom's regret at the thought of postponing his coming to Meldilorn at the Oyarsa's command. "It is not a question of thinking," demurs one of the *hrossa* "but of what an *eldil* says." (XIII). Ransom learned the lesson and thereafter was completely obedient regardless of difficulties.

6. Perhaps the most unusual image in this story is that of the *hnakra*, a word that suggests "snake" and refers to Genesis 3:16. But in this all-but-perfect planet the *hnakra* is nothing more than a real, though deadly, beast and is in no wise a Satanic spirit. To be sure, it sometimes destroys a *hross* but then *hrossa* do not fear death. We are plainly told that Maleldil "let in" the *hnakra* (XII) but also that he is under the command of Maleldil and his Oyarsa (XVIII). We

learn, rather to our surprise, that these beasts are liked and that the very best experience of Hyoi's life was a day in his youth when he went far up to "the place of most awe in all worlds" and stood with Maleldil himself and felt a deepening of his entire life, a day made even more meaningful because the *hnakra* dwelt in the pool below. "There," says he, "I drank life because death was in the pool." (XII) What does Lewis mean? I believe he is suggesting that a safe journey through a dangerous world is better than a mindless trek in a perfectly safe one and that where peril is great the potential for joy is greater. Greater also is the victory of a will which chooses good over evil. The Bible often makes it clear that trials and misfortunes are good for us when properly endured. A U. S. Senator, seeking the cause of crime and decay in today's civilization, suggests it may be our affluent society. "When people feel no need—when they seem to be able to get almost everything they want—they seem to lose something. There's often a lack of gratitude—of appreciation—when things come easily.... no wholesome regard or proper reverence for the true value of life." (*U. S. News and World Report*, March 26, 1973)

7. Augray's discussion of bodies invisible to the eye is an astonishing insight which may approach an explanation of the omnipresence of God. God is everywhere present not like a stolid setting hen but rather as a result of movement rapid beyond our comprehension, so rapid indeed as to be actually "at rest" and without material solidity. Though Ransom thought of *eldils* as being sufficiently ethereal to move through a wall, Augray said that the converse was true—that *eldils* are so solid and real as to pass through a wall as though it were a cloud (XV). Again, therefore, Lewis emphasizes the overwhelming reality of the living God compared to what we ignorantly call reality.

8. Deeply suspicious of much of contemporary "advance" Lewis, in his inaugural address at Cambridge University, sought to identify the period of greatest change in

history. He concluded that it was at the introduction of machinery about 1800 A.D. and that one consequence of the change was a developing notion that moral principles rust out like old machines and need to be replaced by newer ones. Hence our drift from the *Tao*, or universal moral order, into shifting, localized values. One such error was Weston's perfect willingness to sacrifice any number of individual lives in order to bring about the superman who would learn to jump from one dying planet to another and thus acquire endless life. Having no use for anything other than materialistic and scientific values (XX) Weston believed the peoples of Malacandra to be ignorant and backward, yet he had no answer to Oyarsa's query about the superman's fate when all planets had finally died. His view was more quantitative than qualitative. The Oyarsa told Ransom, "My people have a law never to speak much of sizes or numbers (XVIII). Ransom's wrist watch becomes the symbol of how dependant are the people of Earth on measurement (XVII). Weston's philosophy is an example of what Lewis calls chronological snobbery, i.e., the notion that because contemporary knowledge is so great the ancient values may be ignored.

9. In his stories Lewis often depicts someone undergoing subtle temptation from Satan. On his start up to Augray's abode Ransom is forced to make a strong resolution against any changes of mood, but he is shortly beset with an urgent desire to change. Fear and superstition attack him and high up on the steep mountainside in the thin atmosphere he realizes he must either advance or die, so he staggers on (XIV). Where he had felt contented and happy among the *hrossa*, he now felt himself to be in a waste place and completely destitute. The *eldils* and Oyarsa seemed to him mere hobgoblins, or even hallucinations. In his loneliness he even wished for Weston and Devine. Forgetting where he was going and what he was to do when he arrived, yet he went on, thanks to his earlier steady resolution to obey,

and at the top he was rewarded by meeting Augray. Lewis believed deeply in what he called the "old platitudes" and he placed simple obedience high among them.

10. Despite the eldils' supernatural knowledge and abilities such as building space ships, and although their native habitat is in the heavens rather than on planets of any sort, they know only a portion of the bitterest of all stories about Thulcandra (Earth), that is, that once a great and bright Oyarsa ruled there, that he became bent and tried to usurp all power and was therefore punished by confinement to the vicinity of Earth. For the Malacandrians the Earth is the "silent planet," ostracized by sin, and they have only vague reports of how Maleldil there "dared terrible things" (XVIII), i.e., the Incarnation, Crucifixion and Resurrection, to give life and protection to those who would acknowledge his leadership.

11. Lewis associates solemn ceremony with true greatness. Preparatory to the appearance of Malacandra's Oyarsa, the admirable creatures of the land gathered in ritual silence while in the sky hovered a great throng of *eldils*. There is a great difference between the awkwardness and ignorance of Weston and Devine and the ordered and glorious dignity of the occasion. It is a scene reminiscent of Dante's *Purgatorio* or Chapter 21 of the *Revelation*, with some of the glory suggested by a reading of Isaiah 6:1-5.

Perelandra

1. It is not accidental that Lewis chose the planet Venus for this beautiful story, since mythologically Venus has long been the symbol of love. Perelandra is clearly Edenic, a perfect world watched over directly by Maleldil, who "walks" with the Green Lady continuously. So totally pure is Perelandra that a very small lie spoken by Ransom to the Green Lady tore him "like a vomit" (V).

Another resemblance to Eden lies in the one *do-not* command in regard to the Fixed Land on which the Green Lady and her husband were not to remain overnight.

It was because Satan had been confined to Earth, and could not himself travel to Perelandra that he taught Weston the Perelandrian language and sent him as his emissary. In a ghastly scene Weston, now no longer interested in the abstract concept of the superman but a total devotee of emergent evolution and complete submission to the Life-Force, denied Ransom's warning about evil as well as good spirits and opened his being to the demons whereupon Ransom saw Weston's body convulse, fall heavily to the ground and lie as if dead, "a crumbling, a ruin, an odour of decay" (X), acting henceforth as the mere mouthpiece of the Bent Eldil of Earth. Thus a truly devilish evil entered this perfect planet.

One other clear parallel with Eden is Ransom's eventual smashing of the head of the Un-man (his true name, as he had ceased to be a man), while the Un-man in an underwater struggle bit Ransom's heel and inflicted a wound that was not to be healed (Cf. Genesis 3:15).

2. Once again the concept of a universal hierarchy is introduced in a variety of ways. One is the description of the pure glory of the unfallen planet where in the presence of celestial things Ransom realized that all his life hitherto had been lived "among shadows and broken images" (XVII). He saw in Perelandra what he believed to be the true, original model of man and nature—so real and vital that when he returned to Earth his human friend Humphrey seemed to him pale and ill. Ransom, on the other hand, newly arrived from the Edenic environment, was glowing with health and looked ten years younger (II).

Again, Lewis suggests the sad isolation of fallen Earth by uniting all of the rest of the universe with one language (II, XVI).

The Oyeresu of Malacandra and Perelandra contrast radically with our commonly held image of angels as soft and gentle. They presented themselves to Ransom with terrible size and power. Even on this unfallen planet of love they, as heavenly beings, had a verticality that by contrast showed up the planet as somewhat aslant (XVI).

One of the most effective of Lewis's efforts to depict the true nature of Perelandra involves Ransom's inability to describe the reality of his heavenly experience, not because it was in the least hazy but because, on the contrary, it was too definite for Earth's imprecise and limited vocabulary (III).

But it is the Green Lady herself who, by contrast, accentuates our fallen nature most of all. She is at once wise with the wisdom of Maleldil himself and gloriously ignorant of some things. Her very questions give us a stark realization, even an envy, of what it would be like to have her "ignorance." What is peace? she asked Ransom, and what do you mean by "alone" (IV, V)? She herself had never known anything but total peace and the immediate presence of God, those matchless gifts originally intended for man. What is death? was another of her questions (V). Forever replete with the fulness of abundant life, the Green Lady suggests our own fearful emptiness because of ceaseless death in life.

Again Lewis gives us in this story a view of heaven that is, in practicality, almost unknown to Christians. Perelandra is a place not of stodgy or passive contentment but rather of vigorous variety and strength. The Green Lady has full knowledge of her place in a hierarchy where some are above and some below her, and of her proper loving duty towards each. One becomes aware that Maleldil directs all things on this vibrant planet through his immediate presence and yet with no lack of freedom for all its creatures.

On the other hand, with the appearance of the Un-man we see with plangent emphasis what sin has done to Earth. We note the subtlety of Satan's unwearying temptation so that even Ransom, fully aware (as the Green Lady is not) of the situation, is himself shocked and momentarily tempted by the arguments of the Un-man. Theologians have long pointed out that God creates all things good and that evil is a twisting of that good to its own ends. The Un-man's really subtle devilishness was not in trying to make the Green Lady a tragic heroine or in dressing her in beautiful feathers and showing her her own image in a mirror. Rather it was the manner in which he took Ransom's perfectly legitimate assurance that she has a "self," that is, a properly separate identity from Maleldil's, and played his own baleful tune upon such a string. Both of us, said he to her, have come all the way from Earth to do you a great good. Ransom, he went on, has done his part by teaching you of your separateness from Maleldil, and now my part is to show you how you can joyfully demonstrate this to Maleldil simply by disobeying him. He told her how much trouble Maleldil had gone to just to make her own separate identity clear to herself and how he awaited her pushing the button of disobedience that would confirm it and delight Maleldil. It was the "Yea, hath God said?" of Genesis 3:1. But so cleverly and naturally does the Un-man press his point that the reader may begin to feel that he himself might have accepted the Unman's proposition. In many ways Lewis makes it clear that the inveterate call of the self toward its own interests is the key to the Fall of Man.

3. Ransom made the discovery that just as the demonized Weston was the champion of Satan, he was himself chosen by Maleldil and ordered to Perelandra for good in the same way as the Un-man was for evil. Ransom realized that he had no reason for pride, even as Maleldil's agent (II). He was not there merely to witness the situation or to argue, though these functions were appropriate. He was there to act. Heaven was patiently awaiting first his realization and then his action. He was to put all his man-ness into the struggle. His name was Ransom and he was being called upon by Maleldil to ransom this fresh and joyous planet and its two human inhabitants from the curse which had visited Earth. Seeing clearly at last the choice that any Christian must make to stand against evil "principalities

and powers" (Ephesians 6:12), a great clarity spread through his thinking. Its result was that he determined to be obedient and leave the outcome to Maleldil.

4. Obedience is likewise made clear through another image in this story. Like the Green Lady, the Christian is not to live on the Fixed Land but on the floating islands that conform unceasingly to the underlying waves. Whether the water is perfectly still or moving steeply in the storm, one may learn to live calmly and even joyfully on it. "Always one must throw himself on the wave," says the Green Lady's husband (XVII). The Fixed Land may be a set of rules to which one conforms without conviction. It may mean the desire for safety at any price. It may represent the difference repeatedly emphasized by St. Paul to his Jewish compatriots between the Law of Moses and the glorious freedom within the grace of God (Romans 6).

5. In the same connection Lewis supplies us with another astonishing image. Ransom's discovery of it began early in his visit to Perelandra when he found fruit more delicious than any afforded by Earth and when, after he had satisfied his appetite he still wanted more but was somehow withheld from taking it (III). A little later he intuitively rejected a similar strong desire to rush through a whole cluster of the refreshing tree bubbles he had experienced singly. Thinking about the matter, he concluded that this "itch to have things over again" contained some real danger and might even be the root of all evil (VI). Later Ransom heard the Green Lady saying that if one always clings to "the old good" it "would cease to be a good at all" (VI). That she learned this lesson well is indicated in her later remark to Ransom, "We shall meet when Maleldil pleases... or if not, some greater good will happen to us instead" (VII). In this discovery by Ransom and then by the Green Lady, the reader may understand the Scriptural teaching of daily dependence on God and daily expectation from Him of some new value, of looking forward rather than backward,

indeed of recognizing, as Lewis says elsewhere, that actually the only time that is real is *now*. One of my students said that we must not "put *stops* to life" and another observed that "To allow time to become a negative thing is an insult to God." *The Living Bible* paraphrases Romans 12:2, "Be a new and different person with a fresh newness in all you do and think." We are not to vacuum the present by filling it up with either time past or time to come.

6. Nowhere in all of Lewis is the reader lifted up into ecstasy as in the concluding portion of *Perelandra*. The exquisite mountain-top beauty, the coming in heavenly splendor and strength of the Oyeresu, the equally glorious entrance of the now eternally safe Adam and Eve with all their host of loving followers, the ceremonial handing over to them of the planet, and the warm commendation and dismissal of Ransom to return to Earth—all would seem to be indescribable, yet Lewis's extraordinary command of language makes them real to us. Fully as profound is the hymn of adoration to Maleldil, something any Christian might afford to memorize as a permanent fortification of both his mind and his spirit.

7. The following hierarchy and list of planetary names may be helpful. They come from the three volumes of the space trilogy, *Out of the Silent Planet*, *Perelandra* and *That Hideous Strength*.

The Hierarchy:

1. Maleldil—God: the Old One; Glund-Oyarsa, King of Kings

2. Maleldil the Young (or simply Maleldil)—Christ. (The Third One, i.e., the Holy Spirit is mentioned in *That Hideous Strength*.)

3. Oyarsa (plural Oyeresu)—tutelary deity with power from Maleldil to rule. (The name is from the medieval Platonist Bernardus Silvestris.)

4. *Eldil* (plural *eldils* or *eldila*)—an "angel" who lives in space and may visit planets.

5. *Hross* (plural *hrossa*), *pfifltrigg* (plural *pfifltriggi*), *sorn* (plural *seroni*).

6. The Green Lady and her husband the King.

7. Animals.

Names of People:

Tor—King, the Adam of Perelandra.

Tinadril—Queen, the Eve of Perelandra, the Green Lady, *"the* Mother." Tor and Tinadril are also called Baru and Baru'ah, Ask and Embla, Yatsur and Yatsurah, also Oyarsa-Perelendri and Oyarsa-Perelendri-Tor.

Fisher-King—Ransom, later known as the Pendragon of Logres.

Malacandra—the god Mars.

Perelandra—the goddess Venus. At the end of *Perelandra* Ransom discovers these to be the originals of the deities of human mythology.

Edward Rolles Weston (1896-1942)—Scientist later demonized as the Un-man on Perelandra.

Names of Places:

Perelandra—the planet Venus.

Malacandra—the planet Mars.

Arbol—the sun.

Glundandra—the planet Jupiter. (cf. the Glund-Oyarsa above.)

Viritrilbia—the planet Mercury.

Lurga—the planet Saturn.

Tellus (Thulcandra)—the planet Earth.

Numinor (Numenor)—Atlantis, the True West.

Avalon (Abballjin, Aphallin)—island on Perelandra where dwell not only King Arthur but also Enoch, Elias, Moses and Melchizedek. The wounds of Ransom are to be healed there. (Frodo, in Tolkien, who bears resemblances to Ransom, also seems to go there finally.)

Lur—distant spot where Maleldil taught the King of Perelandra many things while the Queen was undergoing temptation via the Un-man.

Tai Harendrimar—the throne, Hill of Life, from which the King and Queen are to reign.

II
Aslan's Country

Narnia was an exquisite valley land created by the great Lion Aslan. Its sun and stars were larger and more brilliant than any in our world. A silvery river ran through its meadows which were filled with the greenest of grass and the brightest of daisies, buttercups and other many-colored flowers. On its little hills were heather and rhododendron, flowering currant and wild rose. There were woodlands and on the ridges, dark firs. Birds filled Narnia with their songs, bees busies themselves with their honey, and a host of butterflies winged their light and easy way in the pristine air.

Up near its northwest corner was Lantern Waste, where the four Pevensie children entered from our world through a magical wardrobe. In its center stood a lamp-post that gave the place its name. Beyond Lantern Waste was a vast cliff from which a mighty waterfall dashed into Caldron Pool, and out from this pool flowed the river of Narnia. Still more westerly lay great mountains covered with dark forests that rose higher and higher divided by deep chasms filled with rushing cataracts of icy water from shining glaciers.

In the center of this mighty western landscape was a sweet smelling valley and a blue lake resting placidly below a hill at whose top grew a garden of beautiful trees with leaves that flashed color as the breeze struck them. At the very center of this garden was a tree bearing great silver apples smelling better than any earthly apples and flashing so bright that instead of shadows they threw light on the green grass below.

To the north of Narnia lay Ettinsmoor with its river Shribble and the wigwam country of the Marsh-wiggles. Beyond that were man-eating giants at Harfang and the City Ruinous, and in the far north lay wild wastelands and great mountains.

Immediately to the south of Narnia lay Archenland whose inhabitants had long been the friends and close allies of Narnia. It possessed its own wooded mountains and one very high peak called Mount Pire, below which a pass allowed travel back and forth. From the southern mountains of Archenland there descended forested hills that slowly gave way to a great desert of sand. Below this desert lay Calormen, the country of a dark-bearded and ancient people who were fond of proverbs, courtly manners and treachery. Its king, called the Tisrock, lived in a grand palace in the center of its glittering capital Tashbaan, named after its god Tash.

The great River of Narnia flowed eastward toward the blue seas where islands stretched to the uprising sun. Like a jewel on this coast lay Cair Paravel, Narnia's high-pinnacled and stately capital. About it one found sweet sands and rocks, the smell of the sea, the call of sea gulls and all the joys of water.

Living in Narnia were both humans and a host of other beings. There were Talking Trees and Talking Animals. There were the Talking Horses Bree and Whin, and Jewel the Talking Unicorn and Mr. and Mrs. Beaver and Trufflehunter the Badger and Glimfeather the Owl and Tumnus the Faun and Moonwood the Hare and Glenstorm the Centaur, and there was the valiant fighting mouse Reepicheep and talking hedgehogs and hares and moles and stags, with many others. Good animals in Narnia might talk as we do, but if they turned bad, as did Ginger the cat, they became dumb.

There were also beings of other kinds. There were Dwarfs, some good, such as Trumpkin and Poggin, and some bad, such as Nikabrik. There were also good and bad giants, and some neither good nor bad, only foolish. And there were strange looking creatures like Puddleglum the Marsh-wiggle, and Dufflepuds and Witches and Efreets and Sprites and Hags. But there were also Dryads and Naiads and Mermen and a Talking Star and bird-girls and larch-girls and river-gods.

Though Narnia was not without dangers, it was truly a place of heart's desire. How could it be otherwise when it was the land of the Great Lion Aslan?

Aslan was the creator of Narnia. This is how it happened. A boy named Digory and his friend Polly, along with Digory's uncle Andrew, a London Cabby and his wife and also a wicked Witch all landed, by magic, in a perfectly empty and totally dark world. As they stared into the blankness they finally began to hear, far off, a quiet tune and at the same moment saw early glimmerings of light by which they could glimpse at a little distance a great golden Lion walking back and forth. It was he who sang, sometimes low, sometimes high, songs that created Narnia. First came a silvery tune that filled the sky with millions of gloriously bright stars. Indeed the stars themselves sang along with Aslan as they came into being. When Aslan sang a louder tune the eastern sky lighted more and more, and as these things happened even the Cabby's horse, along with the others, was tense with excitement, though for Uncle Andrew and the Witch, who were enemies of the Lion, it was an excitement of fear. Now as Aslan sang, a great new sun slowly rose and illuminated a barren valley through which ran a river with hills on either side. In this fresh and pure light they watched the huge Lion, who now sang a softer song. As he walked back and forth green grass dotted with flowers began to spread out from him toward the hills, and heather appeared, and trees. Then Aslan sang again and all sorts of animals, birds and insects began to trumpet, neigh, chirp and buzz.

How splendid, how thrilling this new world was! But how did the evil Witch get there? The boy Digory reluctantly confessed that he was the cause, for earlier, unable to resist temptation even though he had been warned, he had struck a bell that wakened Jadis the Witch Queen who had come with the others to the site of the uncreated Narnia through the power of Uncle Andrew's abominable magic.

So Aslan had hardly completed the creation of Narnia before evil had made its way into it through two human beings. To rectify the error and protect Narnia, Aslan appointed the Cabby and his wife Helen as the first king and queen of Narnia. Then Digory, having made his peace with Aslan, learned of Aslan's intent to plant in Narnia a tree whose odor would be attractive to all true Narnians but repulsive to the Witch and anyone else who was evil. But how was the seed to be acquired? Aslan appointed Digory to mount the Cabby's horse, on whom Aslan had grown splendid wings, and fly far into the Western Wild, there to locate the green hill and its garden and an apple tree in its center. Digory was to demonstrate his repentance by plucking an apple there and carrying it back to Aslan.

With Polly behind him, Digory's long flight brought him to the garden where he entered the high golden gates alone. Inside he found the tree loaded with its glowing silvery apples, and though he was very hungry and longed to eat, he determined to follow Aslan's detailed plan precisely. Just then he discovered the Witch close by. After escaping from Aslan's presence she had climbed over the garden wall. She herself was eating an apple and did all she could to persuade Digory to eat one too. Digory's mother back on earth was ill, and Jadis urged him to carry an apple to his mother and make her well instead of obeying Aslan. What would your mother think, she asked him, if she knew you had such an opportunity and rejected it. When he refused she sneeringly called him the errand-boy of the Lion and a traitor to his mother.

Digory escaped the Witch and on his return Aslan, to Digory's surprise, confirmed her remark that the apple would indeed give daily strength and even greater benefits to the eater, even to the Witch herself. But, said Aslan, she would also suffer endless misery, because people really get what they deeply want even though it may not at all be the best thing for them, particularly if acquired wrongly. When Aslan said "Well done," Digory felt deep satisfaction at having resisted temptation and been completely obedient. The creative power was still effective when Digory, at Aslan's command, threw the apple into the moist earth for it sprang up into a tree loaded with glowing silver apples whose odor made one draw in one's breath with delight. And now, in this gloriously beautiful setting, Aslan instructed King Frank and Queen Helen now to govern Narnia. Guard this tree well, he told all the Narnians, for its odor, so delightful to you, means despair and death to the Witch.

When Digory, Polly and Uncle Andrew returned to earth, an apple from the new tree, brought back by Digory with Aslan's permission, did indeed cure his mother. From its seed grew another tree in Digory's yard and wood from this tree was used in the making of the magic wardrobe.

King Frank and Queen Helen ruled well in Narnia. It was a Golden Age when peace and joy filled the land. Their sons married nymphs and their daughters wood-gods and river-gods. One of their sons became the king of Archenland. Queen Swanwhite, one of their descendants, was beautiful beyond compare. The hare Moonwood in those days had ears so big that he could sit in the far west and hear the least sound on the other side of Narnia in Cair Paravel. King Frank's descendant Gale, ninth in line as king of Narnia, explored the Eastern seas.

It was after this that the Pevensie children of earth entered Narnia through the magical wardrobe. They found it had been winter for a hundred years owing to the evil reign of the White Witch, who had done her best to destroy all the good animals and birds in Narnia and enlisted on her side all the bad ones. Having destroyed or perverted almost everything in her path, Jadis was now queen of Narnia. Because she knew of the ancient prophecy which said that she would die if four "children of Adam" ever sat on the thrones at Cair Paravel, she was naturally determined to prevent any such likelihood.

Thanks to the streak of evil deep in Edmund Pevensie's heart she almost succeeded in making her victory complete. Envious and resentful and even willing to tell lies, Edmund unexpectedly entered Narnia through the magical wardrobe and, coming upon the White Witch, sold himself to her for a piece of Turkish Delight and the promise that if he would bring his brother and two sisters to her she would make him king. The more evil things Edmund did the more he justified them to himself until finally he became an outright traitor, ready to destroy Lucy, Susan and Peter. But they, having also found the way into Narnia through the wardrobe, found a remnant of Aslan's people hiding in deep woods and caves. Delighted at the expectation of the witch's overthrow, they protected the Pevensies and guided them towards the south of Narnia.

Meantime the glorious news began to be noised among his followers that Aslan had returned to Narnia and was on the march. Though the children had never heard that name before, it burned joyfully on their tongues and pierced deeply into their hearts. Getting word of Aslan, the White Witch alerted all her fiendish followers and in her reindeer sleigh drove southwards after the children. But the perpetual winter Jadis had created now began, wonderfully, to take on the warm signs of spring which sent a pang of fear to her heart. By contrast, the appearance of Aslan, the great, golden Lion, filled Peter, Lucy and Susan with joy, and expectation. They loved him at once. Aslan's first task was to gather his faithful ones from their hiding places in which, for generations, they had awaited his return.

At last Aslan came face to face with the Witch and her ghoulish army. In one respect at least she had the law on her side and was determined to see it fulfilled. She held a traitor, required by the law to die, and she anticipated the execution of Edmund with cruel pleasure. To the dismay of some of his followers, Aslan agreed with Jadis that Edmund was properly her victim, and poor Edmund, having discovered a nest of serpents in his heart, hung his head in shame.

When Aslan went aside and talked with Jadis, the children were mystified, wondering how such great good could confer with great evil. Afterwards Jadis walked away with a malignant smile on her face and Aslan with sorrow on his. That night Susan and Lucy could not sleep and went in search of Aslan. They found him in great anguish near a hill on which rested a stone table. Horror stricken, they watched Jadis and a host of her foul followers surround and bind Aslan to the stone. When he was helpless before her, Jadis took a stone knife and, with a shrill shout of triumph, plunged it into Aslan's heart. After gloating over his lifeless body she led her followers triumphantly away, intent now on bringing all Narnia under her control.

Heartbroken, Lucy and Susan made their way to Aslan's body and wept. Unable to untie the knots that held him to the stone table, they were greatly surprised when little mice came and nibbled the cords in two. Then, after the long night of darkness and terror, the light of morning began to appear, and what was their joyful amazement when, just as the sun rose in the east, the sorrowing girls heard a great triumphant shout and looked up to see Aslan alive, more alive, it seemed, than ever. They noticed also that the table on which he had been slain was broken in two right down the middle. Aslan greeted them joyfully and explained what had happened. It was indeed true that the law required a traitor like Edmund to die, but a still older law unknown to the White Witch allowed a willing victim who was free from treachery to die in the traitor's stead. Aslan's death had fulfilled the law, caused the stone table to break and ushered into the world a new and ever-lasting joy.

Now the victorious Aslan, along with the children and all his long-hidden followers, made all-out war against the White Witch, slaying her and releasing her prisoners who, by her wicked magic, had been turned into stone. Narnia grew green after its sterile century of winter and Aslan placed the four children on four thrones at Cair Paravel. There they reigned for many long years with Aslan as their leader, friend and helper in times of trouble. Edmund never again acted in his own selfish interest and served Aslan devotedly.

Then came a day when, in the Western Wild hunting the White Stag (who, if one caught him, would give good wishes), they came again upon the lamp-post and re-entered our world through the wardrobe. They discovered, to their astonishment, that back in the old professor's home no earth time had elapsed and they were again four young brothers and sisters at play.

When next the Pevensie children entered Narnia it was not by means of the magical wardrobe but because of a young Narnian prince's critical need, for Narnia was once again in a most dreadful condition. This was owing to the entrance of a group of earth people through a kind of back door. They had chosen one Caspian as their king, followed by eight other King Caspians. And although Caspian the Ninth was now king, the throne had been usurped by his evil uncle Miraz. Cair Paravel had long since crumbled into ruins and all good animals had been slain or else forced once again into hiding in caves and woods. Some Talking Beasts had even ceased to believe in Aslan.

But young Prince Caspian, despite Miraz' arguments that Aslan and the old Narnia had never existed, firmly believed they did, and in due time he was rewarded by the occasional discovery of Talking Beasts, good Dwarfs and others who had the warmth and joy of old Narnia. Long before, Queen Susan had been given a horn which, when blown in time of trouble, would always bring help. As conditions grew worse and worse and Prince Caspian despaired, he suddenly remembered the horn. Finding it, he sounded a great swelling note that rang out so clear and urgent that it pulled the Pevensies back from their own world into Narnia. There they first found themselves on the very site of Cair Paravel, now in ruins, where they had once reigned as kings and queens. Seeking shelter among the ruins, they managed to open an ivy-covered door and found it led down into the treasure chamber, where they discovered a wealth of Narnian arms and other precious relics of their ancient kingdom.

Feeling sure that they must be needed, they crossed to the mainland of Narnia where they lost their way and for a time were angry with Lucy who insisted that Aslan had called her in a direction different from theirs. Finally they apologized to Lucy when they all met Aslan himself and joyfully realized that he had not really been absent from them at all. Now they were directed to Aslan's How where the armies of Prince Caspian and Miraz had assembled against each other for battle. Nikabrik, a quarrelsome Dwarf on Caspian's side, insisted that to win, they must call up the spirit of the White Witch. Nikabrik also angrily denied that Aslan had ever existed (though at that very moment Aslan stood just outside). In due course Peter challenged Miraz to settle the conflict in single combat. Unable to escape Peter's quick sword, Miraz fell. With Caspian victorious the evil Telmarines in Narnia were sent back to earth through a door Aslan fashioned in the air. The Pevensie children likewise returned and again found that no earth time had elapsed in their absence.

Three years (by Narnian time) after the four Pevensie

children had helped place good Caspian the Tenth on the throne of Narnia, Edmund and Lucy, along with a bullying cousin named Eustace Clarence Scrubb, were magically called back into Narnia for an adventurous sailing trip with King Caspian. It was to take them far away to the utter east of the world. Their ship was built in the form of a dragon with a dragon's head at its prow. The *Dawn Treader*, this beautiful vessel, was loved by everyone except Eustace, who got seasick right away and complained endlessly about everything.

Reepicheep, the gallant mouse, was delighted to go on this voyage. Loving Aslan greatly and wishing always to be near him, Reepicheep was confident that at the very eastern extreme of the world he would find Aslan's country, a place he longed to find with all his heart.

At their very first landing on the Lone Islands their adventures began when they were captured by slavers and led away in chains. Escaping, they discovered that the slovenly governor of the islands had failed for years to pay the required tribute to Narnia and done other evils. After the Prince had disposed of the governor and appointed a good one in his place, they sailed again. A great storm hit the *Dawn Treader* and threatened to sink them, yet they weathered it (though they lost their mast) and landed at what they afterwards named Dragon Island because it was there that the unbearable Eustace, wishing to escape the rest, got lost and, having always thought dragonish thoughts and done dragonish deeds, now actually turned into a dragon.

This was how it happened: When the ship landed Eustace, hating the decency and goodness of the others, slipped away and climbed a high hill. Lying down in the grass, and feeling that at last he was free, he fell asleep. When he awakened he was hungry and decided to return to the ship. But he went in the wrong direction and was horrified to discover, in a deep valley, a dragon crawling out of a cave. It happened to be a very old dragon and, as Eustace watched, it turned over and died right before him. When rain began to fall, Eustace took refuge in the dragon's cave and, being exhausted with his wanderings, again fell asleep. When he woke he remembered with relief that the dragon was dead. But looking down on his left he saw a dragon's claw just beside him. Horrified, he thought it must belong to the dragon's wife. Lying very still, Eustace looked cautiously to his right and to his consternation he saw another dragon's claw on that side.

Then poor Eustace discovered that the claws were his very own, for he had himself turned into a dragon, though with a human mind. He began to review his life, and realizing his dragon tendencies he began to wish to be a boy again, and a good one at that. Finding that (like any dragon) he could fly, Eustace sailed up into the sky and landed near the *Dawn Treader*. Of course the others were quite terrified and prepared to fight for their lives, but Eustace managed to make them understand who he really was. They tried to comfort him, especially the gallant Reepicheep, who had formerly held Eustace in contempt for his selfish ways.

The dragon Eustace was able to help the crew by finding them food and a tall tree for a new mast. Six days later he came back to them in human form and told them what had happened. A great lion which had been following him told him that he must "undress." He remembered that some reptiles cast their skins, so he got a tear started in his own gnarled skin and managed, finally, to pull it all off. He was disappointed to find underneath it another skin just as scaly and black. Once again he tore it and again managed to peel it off but he found *another* tough and ugly dragon skin underneath. Aslan then informed the repentant Eustace that only he could "undress" him. Fearfully Eustace lay down and Aslan (for it was he) put his mighty paw against his breast. The very first tear of Aslan's claw was ever so much deeper than the skin. Eustace was sure it reached clear down to his heart. Yet when Aslan was through

Eustace had become a boy again. Sore as he was, Aslan carried him to a nearby well of water and bathed him. At first Eustace could hardly bear the pain, but soon the icy water made him feel wonderful. Aslan sent Eustace back to his friends a new person. And now the ship itself got under way, but this time with a happy and helpful rather than a cantankerous Eustace.

Their next adventure involved being encircled by a great sea serpent from which they barely escaped. Afterwards they voyaged to an island containing a clear, beautiful lake. On its bottom lay a man who seemed to be made of pure gold. Obviously he had long before thought to bathe in the lake and met his fate there. Then they realized that their own eager intention to bathe there would have been fatal. As they stood on the bank suddenly an angry quarrel arose that later resulted in apologies, and they saw that, beautiful as it appeared, this was a place with a curse upon it. With the help of Aslan they hurried away from a place where pure gold was as common as water but also dangerous as death itself. They called it Deathwater Island.

Next they sailed to the Island of Voices where they discovered a magician who had punished the bothersome Dufflepuds, some silly but friendly creatures, by making them invisible. These Dufflepuds threatened to harm Lucy if she did not slip into the magician's house and discover the spell for making them visible again. Fearfully, poor Lucy tiptoed down strange halls and up suspicious looking stairs and finally found a great, old book with huge metal clasps and vellum pages all handwritten. Her fingers tingled when they touched it.

Lucy turned many pages and saw increasingly real and astonishing pictures and spells. One spell she concluded would make her a great beauty, and she was about to use it when Aslan's face appeared on the page, growling. Next Lucy spoke a spell to see what others thought of her and found herself angry with some of her friends' reactions. But then Lucy found a spell for "the refreshment of the spirit" and discovered herself not just reading but alive on the page. She thought it the finest story she had ever read or ever could read. She continued turning and as she did so she unconsciously became as beautiful as the Lucy she had seen in the book. When she turned to the very best page of all, one containing the real warm Aslan with his golden mane shining, she told Aslan of her joy that he had come and learned that he had been present all the time and that she, by means of the book, had made him visible. Now Lucy was eager to read the story all over again, or have Aslan tell it to her, and he assured her he would do it "for years and years."

Having discovered the spell for making things visible Lucy returned to the Dufflepuds, along with Aslan, and summoned them into view, making them very happy.

Next the *Dawn Treader* came to the Dark Island which was really a dense darkness upon the water. When all agreed on the need to avoid the place, Reepicheep reminded them they were on a voyage of adventure. So in Aslan's name they sailed into the dark, growing more fearful by the moment. Then they heard a voice of terror and took on board a man who urged them to escape quickly, declaring that this was the place where dreams come true, yet dreams filled with dismay. For awhile believing themselves lost in the darkness, they were immensely relieved when they finally saw the light again.

On the next island their adventures included the discovery of a banquet table covered with a crimson cloth and in the center the stone knife which the White Witch had used long before to slay Aslan. At one end of the table they found a number of long-bearded men fast asleep. The sight and odor of the rich food made them hungry and thirsty, yet they feared some danger. Again it was Reepicheep who led the way by climbing onto the table and beginning to eat and drink. They quickly followed his example. Still they were puzzled about how the food kept so fresh. It was Aslan's table, they learned, and the food was placed there day by day for those who really wished to partake of it. The three bearded men had quarreled and refused to forgive each other rather than eat and thus had fallen into a sleep of years while the sumptuous nourishment placed before them daily was left untouched.

After so many strange and often dangerous experiences, and having long been in uncharted seas, the voyagers debated whether to sail farther. Finally agreeing to continue to the east, their fears turned to awe and then to a quiet, deep joy which filled them as sky and sea took on a glory such as they had never known. They found themselves needing less sleep and less food as they went on and their joy grew so deep that they ceased talking at all. Each morning the sun seemed larger and his light created in them a deepfelt ecstasy. It was the sort of light one wished to bathe in. In due course they came upon a silver sea of lilies growing in fresh sweet water and producing a fragrance that filled them with vigorous physical pleasure.

Now they knew they had almost reached the world's end. And here there were sad partings. By orders of Aslan, King Caspian turned his ship westward for its homeward trip. Edmund, Lucy and Eustace were returned to their own world through a hole torn in the sky, also by Aslan's orders, after a meal of fish prepared by a Lamb who changed into the great Lion. Reepicheep had brought along his own little coracle in which he paddled even farther eastward, fully expecting to reach Aslan's own land or else die in the attempt. What great things had occurred to them on this long journey into unknown seas!

The next adventure involved Eustace Scrubb and Jill Pole, pupils at a private school called Experiment House, which they hated. Eustace confided to Jill that during his last holidays he had voyaged on the *Dawn Treader* in Narnia. Once Jill's skepticism about Narnia had ceased, they decided, in their mutual desperation, to hold out their hands to the east and sincerely call upon Aslan. Then, scrambling up a bank they passed through a door in a stone wall. It opened onto a sundrenched meadow dotted with great trees and filled with bird song, while just ahead lay the upper edge of a cliff higher than any in their own world. They had hardly taken in their surroundings before Eustace was blown right over the cliff—blown by a huge Lion, who then walked away. All Jill could do was lie down and cry and feel sorry for herself.

Then she heard the sound of running water and got up and discovered a sparkling stream in a green glade a short distance away. She would have rushed to the water, for now she was very thirsty, except that just this side of the stream lay the Lion. Finally the great beast spoke in a deep golden voice and told her that if she were thirsty she might come and drink. Afraid, Jill could think of nothing except to ask the Lion to go away while she got her drink. Her only answer was a low growl. When she asked the Lion if he would promise not to eat her, he said he would make no such promise. Jill told him she dared not come and he pointed out that in that case she would die of thirst. When, still afraid, but still thirsty, she said she must find another stream, he replied, "There is no other." Finally desperate enough to take a chance on the great Lion, Jill forced herself to go and drink. It was perhaps the hardest decision of her lifetime. She knelt down and with her hand scooped up water which was cooler and sweeter than any she had ever tasted before, water so good that even a little of it slaked her thirst completely. Then the Lion, Aslan himself, called her very close to him and gave her specific instructions to be carried out far below the cliff, in Narnia. Here in the clear air of the mountaintop, he told her, they will seem easy, but down in Narnia the air will thicken and the signs appear different. Nothing else matters, said Aslan, except obeying these instructions. Then he blew Jill off the great cliff and after a moment's fear she began to enjoy herself. Yet even as she floated happily downward she did not forget Aslan's instructions but kept repeating them to herself.

Aslan had told both children how to find Prince Rilian, the only son of King Caspian the Tenth, (who was now a very old man and about to die). A witch had slain Prince Rilian's mother and afterwards Rilian had ridden often into the north to find and destroy the snake, for the witch had taken that form. But the witch could also take the form of a beautiful woman and it was thus she deceived the Prince and seduced him into captivity in her kingdom below the earth. Aslan had instructed the children to find Rilian and bring him back, or else die in the effort. Aslan was not a "tame" Lion and hence might even ask one to give up his life in a worthy task.

So Jill and Eustace landed in Narnia and promptly began to confuse Aslan's signals by forgetfulness and carelessness. When they started northwards they came upon a strange creature called a March-wiggle, Puddleglum by name. He agreed to accompany them and was indeed, despite his inborn pessimism, the best of companions.

Far along in their journey Jill dreamed a dream in which Aslan came and asked her to repeat the signs. Poor Jill had totally forgotten them, and even awake their failure was real enough to land them in the hands of northern giants who intended to devour them as a holiday meal. Now very sorry for their mistakes and desperately afraid, they managed a run for their lives and took refuge in what seemed to be a very small hole in the earth. Small it was, but as it led them down and down it widened into the underworld of the witch and finally into the very stronghold where Prince Rilian was held captive.

The prince explained to them that for one hour each day they must bind him tightly to his silver chair because during that hour he always saw his beautiful captor as ugly and evil. The rest of the time she was his darling. But Puddle-glum and the children discovered the very opposite to be true—in that hour each day the prince was in his right mind and clearly aware of his desperate situation. Part of the enchantment was that for him the truth was reversed. When finally they were able to free Prince Rilian, the witch appeared as a beautiful woman in green. Seeing the situation and intending to capture them, she threw sweet incense on the fire and created drowsy music. At the same time she assured them in soothing tones that there was no over-world of sky and stars and beauty as they supposed but that her underground realm alone was real and they had only dreamed of a better place. The witch's magic overcame Jill and Eustace and almost ovrcame Puddleglum, but just before it did he stamped out the fire. The drowsy incense ceased and their minds began to clear. Thwarted, the witch quickly turned herself into a great, sinuous, green serpent. Prince Rilian himself took a sword and slew her. Afterwards they released many creatures that the Green Witch had made captive and finally made their way back to earth to revel in the real world of stars and sun and other wonders.

Another Narnian adventure took place in the days when the four Pevensie children were kings and queens of Narnia. It began far south in the country of Calormen where a boy named Shasta and a girl named Aravis escaped from slavery and persecution and rode northwards on Talking Horses named Bree and Whin, passing through Tashbaan and thence over the desert into Archenland and finally into Narnia. Actually, a very proud and very silly Tarkaan named Rabadash was determined to marry Queen Susan, and so when Susan and her party made their way out of Tashbaan by a ruse, an army followed them and they had to flee for their lives across the desert to warn of an impending attack, for Rabadash had in mind the extermination of most of the Narnians. By the brave efforts of Shasta the Narnians learned of the matter, gathered an army and totally defeated the Calormene, and Shasta, who had shown princely conduct all along, discovered himself to be the lost son of King Lune and twin to the good Prince Corin.

All through this story Aslan, often unseen, acted as their guide, protector and sometimes chastiser. On more than one occasion it was the much feared roaring of a lion—Aslan, all unknown to them—which put the children and their horses on the right road or prevented them from taking the wrong one. Once, when great speed was necessary to gain safety at the Hermit's house, Aslan caught up with Aravis' flying horse and tore her shoulder with his terrible claws, a horrifying deed which Aravis realized later to be the real cause of her escape from the enemy.

A little later Shasta, who had been sent on ahead by the Hermit into Narnia for soldiers, was walking tired and discouraged along a very dark road when he sensed some being moving quietly just beside him. Shasta's natural fear was gradually overcome as he learned who Aslan was and how he had been their constant companion. He reminded Shasta of that night in the tombs north of Tashbaan when he was afraid of ghosts and how in the form of a large cat he had warmed and comforted him and how later when jackals appeared his roar had stopped their hideous howling out in the desert. As Aslan revealed himself, Shasta grew in understanding and love and finally found it his true duty to fall down at Aslan's feet. Next day he discovered that in the darkness he had been travelling along the edge of a precipice and had been led safely by the great Lion.

And now came a time of degradation for Narnia, brought about by the tricks of a pernicious ape named Shift whose deepest joy was to have plenty of nuts to eat. Regarding Aslan as his greatest rival, he set out to destroy him by a cunning stratagem. First he dressed up a foolish donkey named Puzzle in a lion's skin (which fitted him badly) and exhibited the new "Aslan" to the Narnians in the semi-darkness of a stable door, somehow persuading them, despite their natural good sense, to accept this caricature. Next he allied himself with the Calormenes and invited them into Narnia to cut down trees, even Talking Trees, and engage in commerce. Even worse, he proclaimed that Tash, the god of the Calormenes, was really the same as Aslan, combining the two into a deity he called Tashlan.

This ape managed to capture the good King Tirian and bind him to a tree in the forest. And here, deeply troubled, Tirian called out to Aslan. Thus it was that Jill and Eustace, waiting at an English train station for a train to take them to their schools, found themselves whisked away to the side of Tirian in a Narnia which was no longer the delightful land where the children had once lived as kings and queens. Jill and Eustace untied Tirian and also released Jewel the Unicorn and poor little Puzzle, whom they had captured, and together they began to make plans to outwit Shift and his allies.

The very first group they came upon was a large company of captured Dwarfs being taken to Calormen as slaves. Having first destroyed their guards, King Tirian told the Dwarfs how they had been taken in by the ape. He showed them Puzzle with his donkey head only half covered with the skin and assured them they were perfectly free. But instead of cheers they grinned and sneered and insisted that King Tirian and the children were playing another trick on them. They had been fooled once, they declared, and wished to hear no more stories about Aslan. Yes, they agreed, Tirian had rescued them but he must have some game of his own to play. "The Dwarfs are for the Dwarfs," they declared as they marched away.

Alas, the ape's schemes had been so subtle and far reaching and had swayed so many good Narnians that the oncoming catastrophe could not be prevented. Before a stable on top of a hill the last battle of Narnia was fought and the end came. What heartbreak it was to see the glorious beauty of the land ravaged and every right instinct and action perverted. Bravely as they fought, King Tirian, Jill and Eustace fell in battle. Had not the great Lion Aslan created Narnia, making the stars shine there and grass grow and trees and animals thrive in beauty and joy? Where was Aslan when those who loved him fell before such contemptible agents and all that Narnia stood for was destroyed? Indeed back on earth other tragedies had taken place, for some of the Pevensie children had been killed in the same train wreck which had ushered Jill and Eustace back into Narnia. It almost seemed as though nothing existed but evil; that Aslan, if he was ever real ouside their imaginations, must be dead.

Yet now appeared evidence of Aslan's best plan of all, for the chidren (except Susan who had ceased to be a true friend of Narnia) suddenly found themselves inside the stable surrounded by light and space and joy and dressed in splendid robes as kings and queens of Narnia. And now Aslan himself came to them, larger and more golden than ever, and showed them the last things of old Narnia and then displayed the new unshadowed Narnia into which he led them joyously as they all went higher up and farther in. He told them they were just beginning Chapter One of the final Great Story.

Among the Calormenes who had fought the last battle by the stable was a youth named Emeth who had been a worshiper of Tash, the pagan god. By trickery the ape had caused many of the Narnians to think that Aslan and Tash were one and the same, but young Emeth (for he was no more than a tall, slender boy) believed only in Tash and wanted to serve him fully and if possible to see his face. Emeth had been glad to enter Narnia as a soldier, but was saddened when he learned that the Calormenes were expected to disguise themselves as merchants and overcome Narnia by treachery and falsehood rather than by honorable combat. He was even more shocked when he saw that his own Calormene leaders mocked Tash and did not actually believe in him, and he was convinced that Tash, being a real god, would punish such unbelievers. One of the ape's most devious tricks was to convince everyone that Tash, or Tashlan, was inside the small stable on top of the hill where the great battle was fought. Schemer that he was, the ape did not know that both Tash, the pagan god, and Aslan himself were actually on the other side of the stable door and there each meant to take possession of his own.

Now young Emeth was determined to meet his god Tash face to face, even if he died in the attempt, and so, even as his knees shook, he went with shining eyes and loving countenance through the stable door. But what was his surprise when, instead of darkness, he found himself bathed in sweet and glorious light. He thought this delectable land must be Tash's. But as he went about he saw a Lion so grand and golden and of such unearthly beauty that he fell right down before him, knowing now at once the real truth about Tash and his ungodly followers and aware that Aslan was the one he had truly worshiped as the creator of all that is good. He expected Aslan to strike him dead, but instead the Lion bent over and touched Emeth's forehead, welcomed him and told him that his long search and deepest desire had not been for the lesser but for the Greater. "All find what they truly seek," said Aslan, and Emeth's joy overflowed as he realized that it was the great Lion who had been calling him always.

Thus we have seen the glorious beginnings of Narnia, the various visits made to it by the children, their adventures there and finally its sad end, yet after all not an end for them but rather a great new beginning.

∞

The Narnia stories, as with Lewis's other works, are often more subtle and profound than they first appear. In the following notes I have endeavored to discuss their primary emphases and avoid a detailed or complex analysis.

1. These stories frequently show close parallels with the

Bible, no instance being clearer than that of the creation of Narnia where Aslan is seen bringing Narnia into existence from a "void," not in imitation of the already, sublime account recorded in early Genesis but rather by presenting a warmly creative image in which the great golden Lion Aslan (Christ) sings into existence sun, water, grass, trees, birds—a whole world bursting with life with a mandate to move and breathe and bear fruit. Lewis draws from Job 38:7 for his detail of the stars singing together as part of Narnia's creation. Later in the same story, a fragment of Eden is pictured when Digory is sent by Aslan to the glorious garden far away to procure an apple and resist the enchantment of a temptress who, one notices, has climbed over the wall rather than coming in by the proper gate (John 10:1). The end of Narnia suggests in some ways the apocalypse of St. John the Divine where old things pass away and a new heaven and earth are ushered in. Another clear Biblical parallel occurs in a brief scene near the end of *The Voyage of the Dawn Treader* where Aslan, like Christ with his apostles, prepares a meal of fish for Edmund, Lucy and Eustace before sending them back into their own world. (Cf. John 21:9, 12)

2. Far more common are many implicit parallels, such as the times when Narnia lies seemingly unvisited and uncared for by Aslan and suggesting similar periods in the Old Testament, when Israel through disobedience, experiences the withdrawal of God's blessing. The White Witch kept Narnia in the grip of winter for a century. Aslan's return to Narnia reminds one of the joy and new life portrayed in an Old Testament parallel which describes both the degeneration and the contrasting relief and joy of "spring" returning to Israel, particularly in the books of Ezra and Nehemiah. In both *The Lion, the Witch and the Wardrobe* and *Prince Caspian* we have examples of the "hidden remnant" (Tumnus, the Beavers, *et al.*) who remain faithful even though forced to hide from persecution. Elijah, discour-

aged, informed God that he alone was left and asked God to let him die before he learned of seven thousand in Israel who had not bowed before Baal (I Kings 19:10, 18).

There is also of course a clear parallel between the four signs or rules given by Aslan to Eustace and Jill and the Ten Commandments. The children are instructed by Aslan to obey his instructions in detail, just as God had frequently commanded the Israelites. The unhappy parallel of forgetfulness and outright disobedience is equally clear. Indeed, Aslan told the children that on their mission to rescue Prince Rilian they might lose their lives, a warning which is both literally and figuratively common in Bible history.

3. At a less obvious level there are innumerable Christian implications. In all of Lewis there is no clearer symbol of the unique salvation of Christ and of the inadequacy of self-reformation than in Eustace's futile efforts to cast off his dragon-skin. Only when he submits to Aslan do the Lion's great claws tear off his old nature clear down to his heart and make him new in the well of water. Again Christ as the only way is vividly portrayed early in *The Silver Chair* when thirsty Jill wants to drink but finds the great Lion between her and the stream and realizes that she must drink from this stream or perish. In Eustace's case we are told that it was his continued dragonish thinking which changed the boy into a dragon. In many places Lewis confirms the teaching that the innumerable small decisions of life determine one's direction toward salvation or damnation, a confirmation of the admonition of St. Paul to the Philippians to think on things honest, just, pure, lovely, and of good report (Philippians 4:8).

I had read Lewis a good deal before I fully noticed the beautiful picture of the daily nourishment of the Christian, including the Eucharist, in the rich banquet of food and wine which the children came upon in *The Voyage of the Dawn Treader*. The table was covered with a crimson cloth (the blood of Christ) and on it lay the stone knife which had

slain Aslan. The children learn that such a feast is daily prepared and is to be daily partaken of. Equally significant, the
benefits which God heaps on His people are not dry bread
and plain water but sumptuous and appetizing food. Also
we note that those who will not eat are likely to fall into "a
sleep" and remain essentially dead when they might be
gloriously alive. It seems likely that Lewis had in mind I
Corinthians 11:30 where we are told that some "sleep" because of an unworthy attitude towards the Eucharist. The
gallant Reepicheep, determined to reach Aslan's land or
die, is an example of one not sluggish but responsive and
eager to take part in the Lord's banquet. Reepicheep indeed
has many of the characteristics which identify Aslan—
though at first he is not "tame" toward the despicable
Eustace, it is Reepicheep who quickly visits him and shows
him compassion after his experience as a dragon.

4. As might be expected, there are numerous parallels of
the negative sort, none more shocking than to hear Peter
admit, at the end of the Narnian adventures, that Susan is
"no longer a friend to Narnia" and Eustace, now among the
crowned and glittering ones, adds that Susan had come to
think of all the talk about Narnia as only fanciful childhood
games they had once played. Even from the beginning,
Susan had preferred to be "grown up" and to love the trivial
and second-rate. One recalls how once she seemed to love
Aslan with all her heart. She and Lucy had wept bitterly
when Aslan was slain, and were ecstatic at his resurrection.
Yet a second look shows that all along, Susan was pre-
paring for her final rejection of Narnia by small attitudes
and acts. She preferred to avoid trouble and once made a
list of reasons to leave Narnia when they had only just
entered it through the wardrobe. Minimally, one learns
from Susan's conduct that mere proximity to Christian
things, such as being a church member, is not equivalent
to salvation (Matthew 7:22, 23). The traitor Edmund became
a true follower of Aslan but the toying and hesitant Susan

did not (Revelation 3:15). How many people think, as did Susan, that the magical wardrobe is "perfectly ordinary."

5. Even more specifically, Lewis pictures the meaning of the fall of man and of human sin. Owing to the selfish disobedience of Digory, a witch and an evil magician show up as Aslan's active enemies at the very creation of Narnia. Evil is real and powerful, as evidenced by the White Witch's domination of Narnia for a century. The Witch's tempting of Digory in "Eden" included not merely the fact that the apple was tasty but the subtler claim that if it were taken to his sick mother, rather than to Aslan, it would cure her. She even assured Digory that it would give him knowledge and happiness and everlasting life, promises whose overtones are not wholly dissimilar to Satan's tempting of Christ (Matthew 4:3-11). Edmund's evil ways began with quite minor defects such as a bad temper. And for what shoddy things he sold his loyalty—some sugary candy and the outlandish promise of joining the Witch as ruler over Narnia! The dangers to one who determines to combat Satan are suggested by Prince Rilian, whose intention to slay the witch was reversed when she first captivated him with her beauty and then enslaved him. Witches in Lewis always appear first as extremely beautiful beings. It is only when they are cornered that their essential ugliness is evident. One of Satan's disguises is an angel of light (II Corinthians 11:14). An attack on Satan may become Satan's attack. *The Screwtape Letters* make it clear that what Satan really wants is worldly contentedness and a minimum of concern either about God or himself.

6. Of course, a Christian writer will also picture victory over temptation and sin. In *The Voyage of the Dawn Treader*, before the children carried out their initial plan to jump into the clear and enticing depth of Deathwater, they were forewarned by glimpsing the golden body of a man on the lake bottom and thus escaped his fate. In *The Silver Chair* when the children and Puddleglum were almost completely over-

come by the Green Witch it was Puddleglum, the utter pessimist who always came through in the real pinch, who stamped out the incense fire and turned the witch's own claims upon her by declaring that their supposed imaginary world of free sky and trees and light beat hollow her underworld of darkness and slavery. Fleeing from the giants of the City Ruinous, the children had a "way to escape" (I Corinthians 10:13) even though they found no more than a little hole or crevice, seeming barely adequate in their extremity. But having at last remembered Aslan's commands and confessed their errors, they found it so much more than a bit of hole—they found it the entrance to the Green Witch's underworld and the beginning of her destruction and Prince Rilian's release. Puddleglum had told them, "Aslan's instructions always work: there are no exceptions," and now they saw a little escape hole turned into an avenue of final victory.

7. Of course the most splendidly persistent Christian image in the series is that of the Lion Aslan. Often Aslan is represented as being immediately present, whether seen or unseen, as with Shasta and Aravis, and as guide to the children. He is the only salvation, the answerer of prayer, the creator of true joy, the sovereign in his universe. We are told repeatedly that he is "not a tame lion." He is at once more powerful than his adversaries and also the essence of charity. "You would not have called to me," Aslan told Jill, in *The Last Battle* "unless I had been calling you." He is always aware of the demands of the Law, as seen in his death for another on the stone table, a confirmation of Galatians 3:13, "Christ hath redeemed us from the curse of the law, being made a curse for us." But he is greater than the Law. "For what the law could not do ... God sending his own Son in the likeness of sinful flesh, and for sin, condemned sin in the flesh." (Romans 8:3). And all this was the Deeper Magic about which the White Witch knew nothing for it had been "foreordained before the foundation of the world." (I Peter 1:20).

The Narnia stories often picture the winsomness of Aslan and his gifts. The exquisite beauty of Narnia with its clear streams, its waterfalls, its Edenic garden containing silver apples and leaves that cast a supernatural light, and its entrancing fragrance is an important example of the pleasure these stories give old and young readers. As to odors, Lewis is almost unique in emphasizing this poignant Biblical image. The account of the tree planted in the new-made Narnia with its smell which is "joy and life and health" to the children and "death and horror and despair" to the Witch is an almost direct parallel to II Corinthians 2:15: "For we are unto God a sweet savour of Christ, in them that are saved, and in them that perish: to the one we are the savour of death unto death; and to the other the savour of life unto life."

8. Emeth, in *The Last Battle*, has troubled some readers. Lewis is by no means saying through Emeth that sincerity is all that God demands. To suppose this is to contradict the whole tenor of Lewis's Christian works. Young Emeth was a desperate seeker after the truth, ready even to die for it, and he had wrongly supposed that it resided in Tash. His eye was fixed on something nobler than most of us could claim—but Tash, for a while, stood between him and Aslan. When he finally came into the presence of Aslan he recognized his true Master and instantly and abjectly renounced Tash, praying for Aslan's forgiveness. Aslan told Emeth that everything good belonged to him, everything evil to Satan, and recognized that Emeth's eager search had been for the truly good. Had not Aslan called the selfish Eustace out of his dragonhood and had he not called the traitor Edmund, and why should he not call one utterly given to the search, however awkwardly, for the great Lion himself? Aslan had told some of the children how they were brought into Narnia to learn his "other" name (*The Voyage of the Dawn Treader*, XVI). Emeth also learned it. Indeed it was Lewis's hope that all his readers, as they followed the

adventures of the Narnian world, would learn Aslan's real name. At the very end of *The Voyage of the Dawn Treader* Aslan told Edmund and Lucy that from all worlds there was an entrance into his country.

9. The ape's devilish ability, in *The Last Battle*, to lead everyone astray seems to represent the result of living in a pragmatic, materialistic civilization in which even many Christians turn cold and unbelieving. Lewis, as always, depicts in the Narnia stories the tragedy of religious liberalism, one instance being the bag of tricks by which Aslan is identified with the pagan god Tash and a grotesque lion's skin awry on an innocent donkey is taken as explicit reality. Like Prince Rilian in the hands of the Green Witch, people may actually become oblivious to their own best welfare except for one hour in every twenty-four. How many hours each day am I really sane, how many do I spend unaware, facing in the other direction?

Lewis's decision to complete the seven Narnia books with the destruction of Narnia may be seen as nothing more than a literary device. But I doubt that this was his intent. More likely he is joining the image of what he regarded as a clearly degenerating civilization arriving at its inevitable end with the Biblical record of an apocalypse and afterwards "a new heaven and a new earth." (Revelation 21:1.)

10. We are told that the old Narnia had a beginning and an end and that it was only a shadow of the Narnia "in Aslan's real world." This suggests Luke 1:33 and the kingdom of Christ which is to be endless and without need of further reconstitution.

11. The blind obstinacy of the Dwarfs in *The Last Battle* suggests people who, having been once trapped by a set of circumstances, resolve never again to be trapped by either good or evil and simply board themselves up with lifelong bitterness and cynicism, or at least indifference.

12. There is much in chapter XIII of *The Last Battle* about blindness and sight. Like the Dwarfs who were totally un-

able to see the beauty around them, the Calormene sta-
tioned inside the stable door was blind to the children. On
the other hand, Emeth, loving the truth and seeking it with
all his heart, could see. The Bible often speaks of the blindness of people who have nothing wrong with their eyes
but much with their spirits, as in Matthew 15:14.

13. The great and ancient book which Lucy found in the
house of the old magician in *The Voyage of the Dawn Treader*
is in many ways like the Bible. In it, Lucy found a "spell"
to make even Aslan visible and present, though Aslan had
to inform her that he really had been present all the time.
She found spells for the refreshment of the spirit but none
to simply beautify one's body. Again she found pictures in
the book that made her weep and repent of evil. Then we
learn that as Lucy continued turning the pages and taking
note of the contents of the great book she herself unconsciously grew more and more beautiful. What a strong confirmation of Lewis's belief about the authority of the Bible
and also of its power to transform one's life from the ugliness of sin to the beauty of the Lord God (Psalm 1) but only
as it is continuously and carefully perused.

14. In the Bible, the impartation of some particularly
great gift may be accompanied by a "breathing" upon its
object, and this image is paralleled in the Narnia stories.
The children were pierced with tingling joy at the very last
act of Aslan's creation of Narnia, when he breathed out "a
long, warm breath" upon his creatures and in his deepest,
wildest voice called on them to think and speak and live, an
act which suggests the vivid account of Ezekiel 37:1-10 and
especially verse 9. In *The Lion, The Witch and The Wardrobe*,
Aslan breathed on the animals and Dwarfs which the White
Witch had turned into stone and brought them back to life.
He also breathed on Emeth after his abject confession of
obedience. All these acts remind us of our Lord's breathing
on his disciples in John 20:22.

15. C. S. Lewis sets forth in clear imagery the direction

and rewards of the Christian way. For instance, the portion of his autobiography which he completed has, as the heading of its last chapter, "The Beginning," meaning that he was then starting out as a newborn Christian. Years later he called the last chapter of *The Last Battle* "Farewell to Shadow-Lands" and said that the children, now having died, were beginning "Chapter One of the Great Story . . . which goes on for ever: in which every chapter is better than the one before." (XIV)

16. At the end of *The Last Battle* the children saw all the inhabitants of Narnia in vast numbers come to a doorway where stood Aslan and, after looking intently at him, split into two groups. One group, loving the face of the Great Lion, entered through the Door. The others, full of fear and hatred, swerved away from the Door and disappeared into a great black shadow (XIV). This is clearly the imagery of Matthew 25:31ff. Jesus called himself "the door." (John 10:9)

King James

III
Malevolence
in Action

The Screwtape Letters

In the infernal regions below his Abysmal Sublimity, Screwtape, the Undersecretary, carries on a busy correspondence with his nephew Wormwood, the Imp. Wormwood is assigned as hellish caretaker of the soul of a young man just on the point of becoming a Christian. All hell, indeed, is a busy place where innumerable wheels turn and tempters hurry here and there in abject haste to defeat the great Enemy above. Hell has its High Command and its Infernal Police and a House of Correction for Incompetent Tempters. Although none of the members of the Lowerarchy are free from pain, particular clumsiness brings its own stinging reward, for hell hates inefficiency as well as equality and is a place of everlasting jealousy, politicking and blackmail.

What hell wants most is food, for it goes hungry in the presence of goodness and its greatest hope is for a feast over a human soul lost to heaven. Thus hungry Screwtape keeps in close touch with Wormwood and requires numerous progress reports from him.

Indeed Wormwood is from the outset in serious trouble with his uncle, for his young charge has turned to Christ and immediate action must be taken to reclaim the patient, as he is called. Remember, writes Screwtape by way of encouragement to Wormwood, that no settled devotion to the Enemy has yet occurred and the patient still retains his old patterns of thought. Screwtape notes that although the Enemy could make this young fellow instantly into a real saint full of charity and overflowing love, that is not His method. He has the very unhellish idea of letting him contribute to his own upward growth. So the way is open to hell to create in him, on the one hand, questions as to what a Christian really is and, on the other, feelings of pride that he is now a follower of the Enemy. Everything possible must be done to make his prayers conventional and dry, not the outflow of his own deepest hopes and trust.

Learning from Wormwood of weaknesses in the patient's mother, Screwtape happily urges his nephew to work closely with her tempter Glubose to cause the patient, even as he prays for his mother, to be irritated by the memory of the faults, facial expressions and accents that he long ago learned to dislike in her; also to see if anything can be made of differences on religious issues between her and her son. Though prayer is always in the Enemy's favor, it has its own possibilities such as causing him simply to parrot his childhood or church prayers and also making him regard his prayers as successful on the basis of feelings rather than any direct communication between him and the Enemy. The main idea is to prevent his ever genuinely baring his soul before the one he calls the Great Omnipotent God.

Next, Wormwood writes of his delirious happiness because another War has started. Screwtape greets this with surprising moderation. To be sure, he agrees, wars are an encouragement to hell, but they also have their dangers. Wars bring on tribulation, but tribulation can do as much for the Enemy as for us because it causes our patients to think about serious matters in both public and private life, whereas we want always a contented worldliness. War also encourages thoughts about death, something quite contrary to our best interests. We encourage the assumption that death is still a long way off. To our chagrin, our Enemy tells His children that suffering is a ladder upwards to staunch faith. Anyway, Screwtape adds, even if faith could be destroyed by war or pestilence, we in hell are deprived of the choice pleasure of watching in our patients a slow disintegration of belief.

Learning from Wormwood that the patient may be enlisted for war service, Screwtape urges him to keep the young man's mind in a state of confusion and never allow him to conclude that these uncertainties are the appointed cross he is to bear but rather uncalled for interruptions in his private affairs. He urges Wormwood to make unreal to his patient everything genuinely spiritual and attack his patient's central, heartfelt will.

Asked by Wormwood whether he is to keep his existence a secret from the patient, Screwtape advises that the present policy of hell is concealment. Naturally hell, for its own pleasure, would prefer to terrorize directly. The trouble is that when humans really believe in hell they are on their guard and make hell's work far more difficult. Fortunately, says Screwtape, we have given most people nowadays the image of ourselves as comic figures in red tights, a stroke of real genius.

What Screwtape really wants is disbelief in the great Enemy. Any extremes—except of course extreme devotion to the Enemy—lead toward disbelief provided they are as violent as possible—extremes, for instance, in patriotism or pacifism. "Inner circles" are also desirable from hell's view, and much can be given to the netherworldly cause by a church which by fear and defensive self-righteousness isolates itself from the loving service to which it is called. The real trick, whatever the patient's extremism, is to let him substitute it for real belief in the Enemy, to involve him in busy work such as committees and localized crusades that wean him away from steady devotion and good works.

Now Wormwood reports happily to his uncle that apparently the patient is losing his faith. Screwtape angrily retorts that his nephew has failed to profit from the Training College of hell and asks him if he has never heard of the law of Undulation. Never forget, he writes, that all patients are made up of a body and a spirit. The spirit is addressed to the Enemy but bodily functions always undergo high and low periods. The patient's present arid period is doubtless temporary. The truth is that our purpose is slyly to steal full possession of the patient's will. The Enemy wants the very opposite—instead of absorption, as with us, He has the strange ideal of humans making free use of their will to grow into His likeness. His plan, so different from ours, is to let them become one with Him and simultaneously keep their own freedom and personality. It is a dreadful thing for us, he continues to Wormwood, when a patient, established in obedience, continues to pray and to trust while momentarily forced by his feelings to suppose that our Enemy nowhere exists. What we want is moderation in religion. We know that when that is well established in a patient he is ours. Always our best hope is to nudge out of him any clear distinction between the true and the false and keep his belief hazy all his life.

Screwtape and his understudy are delighted when the patient makes the acquaintance of a couple of worldlings owned by hell who introduced him to their whole set. Now, says Screwtape, the patient must be encouraged to drift into their circle and adopt their bright skepticism. Let him pretend to be like them and he will indeed become like them, first in their presence and afterwards wherever he may be. Or perhaps he can be brought into a hypocritical position of endeavoring to follow two different directions, maybe even enjoying the paradox. Let him, ideally, become merely flippant. It favors us even if he continues church attendance and prayers and regards his compromising conduct with his new friends as only a phase. In this position he will find no need to repent from his real sins. He will be moving toward our goal and perhaps discover at last that he has done neither what he ought nor what he liked.

But such a hope is dashed and poor Wormwood is forced to report a real repentance and renewal in his patient. Incensed, Screwtape reviles him as an amateur tempter. Why did he ever let his client have a quiet walk alone through countryside and have tea at the old inn and read a book that he genuinely enjoyed? Real pleasures, he tells Wormwood, are most dangerous. What we want is for our clients to "be somebody" inside the reigning circle. Our policy is never to let anyone do anything for its own sake but rather use everything to enlarge the ego.

And now comes very bad news indeed. The patient has not only abandoned the reigning clevers but has resolved to be daily, even hourly, dependent upon the Enemy. Now, advises Wormwood, the very thing you should have avoided has come upon us. Your patient has arrived at a state of genuine humbleness before the Enemy. All we can hope for now is his pride at being humble. Or maybe we can persuade him to demean his true talents by giving him a false sense of real dignity and real ability. All such exercises succeed by making the patient's mind revolve about himself rather than looking objectively to the Enemy and obeying Him.

On learning that the patient has settled down as a regular member of the parish church, Screwtape urges efforts to make him critical and send him out to other churches looking for something more to his liking. Ideally, he should be led to a nearby church in which the clergyman waters down the Christian faith to make it more palatable for the moderns, then to another church where the clergyman preaches only to puzzle or shock and builds his sermons upon hatred rather than love.

Nothing troubles Screwtape quite as much as what he calls the vulgarity of the Enemy, who really *loves* "human vermin" which hell regards as fit only for its own fun and food. Why, for instance, did He make sex a good and joyful thing that encourages quiet family life and the impulse to produce children as part of a unity of trust and compatibility? Hell hates the Enemy's grand scheme to make people his own free and loving children. On the contrary, says Screwtape, hell has dignity and position, while the Enemy, having no dignity, gives His people a warm relation to Him through praise and prayer and when He sees these clods on their knees He reveals Himself and gives them heavenly knowledge and spiritual joy. Hell's intention, by contrast, is to absorb people. The Enemy wants to make humans more than human. He is bourgeois and simplistic in filling the world with pleasures and promising, after death, even greater ones. .

In truth, insists Screwtape, the Enemy has left nothing naturally on hell's side, so to gain our ends we must twist everything. He gave pleasures and so we must create a craving for pleasures which diminish as they are enjoyed. He has given music; what we want is noise—ruthless, unceasing noise. He has given them a fragrance most pleasant to the kingdom above but deadly to us. He has filled their world with beauty, while what we want is everlasting distortion. He has given them appetites and food to satisfy it, therefore we must turn appetite into gluttony. He has made them love the platitudes of life which we must twist into a passion for newness, up-to-dateness and eccentricity. All His positives we must turn into negatives. Even His gift of time we must twist either into melancholy memories of the past or fearful anticipations of the future.

He has ordered them to obedience and rewarded those who practice it. Virtue, that most obnoxious thing to us, He allows them to practice joyfully. While we suffer everlasting agony, He has taught His people to embrace pain as a means to educate and purify their souls. Because our Father Below hates nothing more than *mere* Christianity, our everlasting task is to make it fuzzy, complicated and unacceptable.

And now comes word that the patient has fallen in love, and with whom? A virgin and Christian and one from a home equally detestable, reeking of that odor deadly to hell! It makes Screwtape want to vomit. In fact, he is so angry that he turns temporarily into a centipede, and Toadpipe, his secretary, has to complete the letter.

Screwtape informs Wormwood that something desperate must be done and proposes inculcating variations on faith itself by creating another "historical Jesus" of the sort that varies with each generation, each as warped from the truth as the last. The real Jesus of the sacraments, the object of genuine devotion, must be changed into a shadowy, remote and to all intents obsolete being impossible to worship—simply another great man. Instead of the resurrected Christ who convinced the disciples and made them into persuasive witnesses, and often martyrs, Screwtape suggests the creation of a new "vogue" Jesus, attaching to Him slogans such as social justice and making Him a means rather than an end.

Into the patient's courtship, seeds must be sown that will spring up years from now as resentments and hatreds. The patient is fervently in love now and supposes that it will always continue thus, not knowing that another and deeper permanent love will follow provided he and his beloved practice the Enemy's intentions of sacraments and charity. We must take advantage of this and turn them at the proper time to bitterness. Let them come to "live for each other" in such a twisted manner as to result in constant irritation and hidden grudges on the one hand and what they call self-sacrifice on the other.

Screwtape gives advice concerning the patient's prayers. If he prays for a sick friend and that friend dies, then remind the patient that his prayers simply did not work. If the friend recovers, assure him that it was owing to the skill of the physician. Or remind him that the immutable Enemy knew everything from before time began, even the very words the patient would speak, so why should he pray anyway? He is probably not knowledgeable enough to understand the part played by prayer in the Great Dance of time and eternity.

Wormwood writes glowingly of the death and destruction which the war is creating and informs Screwtape that it is likely the patient's own town will be bombed. But don't you see, Screwtape reminds him, that while hell naturally loves war, in this case a Christian is involved who may die in the bombing, precisely the thing to be scrupulously avoided. Disgusted with Wormwood, Screwtape lists his failures. He did not prevent him from giving up his fashionable friends nor from falling in love with a Christian girl, and now he is busy with the dangers and responsibilities entailed by war and thus the chances to reach him grow less. Indeed, the Enemy has effected in him, as in humans generally, a deep longing for eternal things that we cannot finally erase. Wormwood must do something, and in a hurry; search for ways to confuse the patient, fill him with fear, make him a coward, let him do his duty shakily rather than with assurance, make him short tempered, create irritations on every hand. Make him suppose the terrors of war are real events and the happiness of children at play is mere sentiment.

Then comes the fatal word that the patient has died suddenly in a bombing raid. Because a soul is thus lost to hell, Screwtape promises Wormwood he will pay dearly for his failure. To torture him, he describes to Wormwood exactly what happened to the patient. One moment there was all the confusion of war—the crash of falling bombs, the stink of explosives, the collapse of buildings. Next moment every problem of life was wiped out and the patient suffused with ecstasy. He saw the Solid Ones of heaven, spirits before whom we can only cower, and instantly he knew them not as strangers but as the true source of his lifetime longing and the heart of every true experience. Furthermore, said Screwtape, this creature, this thing born into the fallen world which it has been our business to corrupt, this young man saw Him. He saw the great Clarity and He was in the form of Man. The cool light shed by His presence which would blind and suffocate us is now the celestial reward of a mere man.

Screwtape concludes by berating the poor management of hell for such failures as the present one, by wondering how the Lowerarchy will ever finally discover what the Enemy is really up to, and, surprisingly, by dropping a hint that he is himself tempted to give up to the Great Enemy, but not before poor Wormwood has become a dainty morsel for the hungry jaws of hell.

∞

The Screwtape Letters is easy reading, though not quite as theologically uncomplicated as it might seem at first glance. Attention may be called to a few things.

1. We recognize in this work Lewis's clear and incisive knowledge both of the Scriptures and of the subtle points of neglect by which the Christian fails to practice "mere" Christianity.

2. This book could hardly have been written except by a man who truly believed in the reality of God and of Satan and who was genuinely concerned that we avoid evil at all costs and adhere to the daily calling of God.

3. We find here Lewis's steady objection to religious liberalism and his orthodox view of the Incarnation (IV), the Resurrection (XXIII), the Trinity (XVIII), the Fall and Satan's removal from heaven (XIX), repentance (XII) and conversion (XIII).

4. As might be expected, Lewis holds up the life of rational orderliness as superior to reactions based on feelings, though of course he does not exclude emotion. Lewis believed and convincingly demonstrated that our age, in spite of its claims to the contrary, is not one that reasons well.

There was an earlier time when men directly connected reason with action (I) so that what they concluded to be right they tended to put into practice, but the coming of superficial "jargon" into the world has pretty well erased that danger to hell. We now prefer the sophisticated and shrewd (X), reading "important" books so that we may casually make it known we have read them (XIII) and satisfy our ego by joining as many inner circles as we can and bragging, outwardly or at least inwardly, about "our set" (XXIV). We wipe out the great truths of the past not by seriously asking whether or not they are still true but by researching into recent opinions on them (XXVII). We have discarded the fundamental moral order of the universe and substituted our own localized morals (XXIII). Even the arts are now not dangerous to hell (XXV) and science, which is friendly to true Christianity, has been made its enemy (I).

5. Though God appears here as sovereign he is, from hell's point of view, bourgeois, even vulgar. He really loves the race of men and wants to restore them to the kingdom of heaven not by magic or force but by their free will. God has filled the world with pleasures, while hell hates laughter and all the pleasures of beauty and proportion and true perspective.

6. The Holy Spirit is seen by hell as an "asphyxiating cloud" about the patient (XIII) and the most successful defense of the Christian against temptation. "Some human beings," admits Screwtape, "are permanently surrounded by it and therefore inaccessible to us."

7. Perhaps the passage of Scripture which most directly parallels *The Screwtape Letters* is our Lord's parable of the sower in Matthew 13:18ff.

8. As usual, Lewis ends on a note of high drama by having Screwtape from his place in all the shoddiness and selfishness of hell describe for Wormwood the glorious death of the Christian and his entrance into heaven.

IV
The Everlasting
Incorrigibles

The Great Divorce

The longest busride ever began with a waspish, scowling, growling, pushing queue of people which had established itself in the rain on a shabby street in the twilight of a city where in every direction one could view nothing better than dingy streets presided over by an eternally leaden sky.

When the bus came into sight it put to shame all other buses that have ever been. It was alive with golden light and heraldic color and clearly belonged to some other realm than the dreary diabolism abounding here. As the bus stopped, the quarreling queue turned its attention to the Driver, who was radiant enough to seem like light itself. Yet as they fought for places (although indeed there were plenty for all) they flung caustic remarks at him. Mainly they wanted the Driver to be a "good guy," a regular fellow like themselves.

While some of the passengers continued to wrangle and sometimes break into outright blows and some to justify themselves by demeaning others, the glorious vehicle rose above the roofs of the vast grey city. Over the houses and upward it traveled until, a long time later, a slow light began to appear, growing into a radiance that dazzled eyes long used to the dim land below and revealed faces sadly disgruntled and distorted. A cliff finally appeared ahead and above it a green landscape with a wide river through its center. Here the bus landed and the passengers, still pushing and cursing, made their way out.

Now the everlasting twilight of the grey city was replaced by the cool intimate light of a summer sunrise. Even from a distance the landscape seemed more than geography but rather the whole proper universe itself. A lark's song broke the stillness and a warm joy, tinctured also with some sense of danger, hung in the atmosphere.

And now as the passengers began cautiously to move about their new environment, two astonishing things became apparent. Their bodies which, in the grey city, had seemed quite normally solid and real were here transparent against the chaste brightness of the light. They had become ghosts. The other strange thing was that for the bus people the landscape contained objects of such amazing solidity that, although birds easily bent the grass or twigs they landed upon, to the feet of these passengers the same grass was as hard and sharp as diamonds and lifting even a small leaf became a back-breaking task.

One passenger soon turned to the Driver and asked when they would be allowed to return home. He was told that they could remain here always if they chose. They could, if they wished, exchange their twilight land for this unexampled glory, and only the genuine wish not to do so stood in their way.

These poor stumbling ghosts also glimpsed a distant range of great mountains with cities on some of the highest peaks and saw, far off, bright beings coming towards them. As these approached they proved so brilliant with joy that some of the ghostly ones ran, as best they could, for shelter. But not all, for some of the insubstantial ones, unmoved by the momentous events in which they were involved, took advantage of their situation to argue the superiority of their decisions in the seamy events of their earlier lives and the misery they had managed to create. Others sought logically to prove that there can be no life after death. Some even offered to take over this newly discovered land and lay claim to it as an extension of their own great domain below. A few could only creep around defeated, spitting out their contempt.

With courtesy and grace the Solid Persons approached this passenger or that and, with expressions and actions redolent of the glad reality of their true universe, proffered to each a warm invitation to come and live forever in the delectable mountains over which the sun was rising.

One bright Person approached the Big Man who was his employer on earth. As they talked, one was felicitous and full of earnest joy, the other hostile and increasingly angry. The Bright Person readily confessed that on earth he had murdered another employee but explained that here both he and the murdered one now live in the ecstasy of the mountainous country; indeed, that the murdered one had sent his love. Blustering, the Big Man refused obstinately to understand why he must live in the pigsty of the grey city while a murderer enjoyed this place of light. Admitting that he was not a religious man, he protested that he had, nevertheless, done his best all his life. All he wanted was his rights.

But, explained the Bright Person, this is not a country in which one ever gets his rights—he gets something far better. The Big Man remained shocked at the incongruity of a murderer being given benefits which he, a blameless citizen, was deprived of. "I only want my rights," he repeated. "I'm not asking for anyone's bleeding charity." "Then do. At once," said the Bright Person, "Ask for the Bleeding Charity."

The Big Man boasted again about the decency of his life and demanded its proper reward. "But neither you nor I," said the Spirit, "were really decent, nor did we do our best. I murdered Jack in a moment of anger, but for long years I lay awake at night murdering you, my employer, in my heart. And you know very well that you were neither a kind employer nor a thoughtful husband and father." Insulted, the Big Man swore at the Bright Person, declaring he would never come to the mountains with a murderer and snivelling for charity. "I'll go home. Damn and blast the whole pack of you." And so with a grumble and a whimper the Big Man made for the bus.

Near the wide river flowing across the landscape came another Bright Person to a fat, clean-shaven man with a cultured voice, none other than a ghostly Episcopal Bishop. Unlike the Big Man, the Bishop's conversation remained suavely genial. Finally told plainly that he was an apostate, the Bishop insisted he was rather a man of honest though liberal opinion, a hater of what he called "prejudice" and "stagnation." Had he not demonstrated his intellectual integrity by rejecting, when it ceased to convince him, the doctrine of the Resurrection of Christ? Indeed, said he, the very sermon enunciating his more up-to-date belief had been delivered to his congregation at great risk to his position and reputation. On the contrary, said the Bright Spirit, it was that sermon which had actually gained him popularity and a bishopric. Indeed, the Bright Person continued, even in his school days he got into the habit of writing essays to please his instructors and fell into dishonest thinking that catered always to the prevailing winds, almost never voicing an opinion arising out of verity and singleness of heart. He came to love points of view better than he loved God. Now that he had experienced both the grey world below and seen the glory of this one, would he not face the truth and come where he could be made white as snow? But the Bishop continued to bandy theological terms as the Spirit earnestly invited him into the land of Eternal Fact where answers replace speculations and where one might taste truth like honey and see the face of God.

Insisting that he preferred to search rather than to find, the Bishop remained unmoved. Suddenly he remembered that he must deliver a paper to his little theological group in the grey city, a group which needed him because they tended to be jealous, ill tempered and confused in their thinking. He hoped to encourage them with a paper on Jesus and how, had he not died so early, his mature views might have promulgated a better Christianity. What a tragic waste, lamented the Bishop, was the crucifixion, and with a last flash of his bright clerical smile he started for the bus.

Now the onlooker came upon a very tall man with a flowing beard sitting on a large smooth rock near some pines. A man? No, but rather a shining Spirit looking like a shepherd of great honesty and thoughtfulness. It was George MacDonald. The onlooker asked him many questions about this country and the grey city below, about Reality itself and about choice and why so many would not accept Joy. MacDonald answered that it is because "there is always something they insist on keeping, even at the price of misery." They demand their own will above everything else in the universe. Self-choice, said he, is the rock on which they founder.

As they walked about MacDonald allowed the onlooker to observe other encounters. One was between a Bright Spirit scattering light from his hair as he approached a Ghost who in life had been a famous artist—a Ghost bemoaning his failure to bring along his paint and brushes. Conversing, the Bright Person disclosed that he would be able to paint here only after he had first "grown into a Person." The painter confessed that he had once built his paintings around light but that he outgrew all that and developed paint for its own sake. That is the great danger, said the Spirit, to anyone who becomes a creative artist. As he gains a reputation he may turn away from his first and proper love into cleverness, eccentricity and the display of self. Almost persuaded, the artist allowed the Spirit to take his arm and lead him a few halting steps in the direction of the mountains, but then stopped to inquire whether he should not meet and join a coterie of other famous painters in the mountains ahead. All are now equally famous, he was told, made so in the Great Dance rather than by their accomplishments, made famous indeed by the Light. Well, said the Ghost, disappointed, I shall have to be satisfied with my earthly reputation. To his consternation he learned from the laughing, joyous Spirit that their paintings (for the Spirit was once an artist himself) had long since been forgotten because of changing fashions. The painter, now thoroughly disgusted, would not hear another word but rushed away, intent on delivering a manifesto and starting a movement—anything to regain name and reputation, to be Somebody, a motive which had increasingly dominated him and now did so with such completeness that not even the presence of the Bright One made any differnce.

And now as the onlooker and MacDonald went about they saw, for the first and only time, a Bright Person of blazing light succeed in his invitation to a Ghost, dark and oily in appearance, who was talking to something it carried on its shoulder, a little red lizard of lust. Though the man hated the lizard it managed nevertheless, by its chatter, to control him most of the time. But the onlooker noted that here was a Ghost truly wanting to be rid of his incubus, not to "explain" it and hold on to it. Shall I make the lizard quiet, asked the Bright Person, and the Ghost readily assented. But he had not expected anything so drastic as the Angel's quick movement to kill the lizard. Look, he said, it's gone quietly to sleep and can be managed. Talking rapidly to the Spirit, he asked for time and offered palpable excuses. The Angel drew closer and the lizard wakened and whispered a torrent of warnings and promises into the man's ear. At last the ghost, in desperate turmoil, shouted his wish to have the thing over with. He screamed as the Spirit, whose flaming nearness burned him, grabbed the biting, twisting lizard and flung it against the earth. Overwhelmed, the Ghost gasped and reeled.

And then three things happened quickly. First the Ghost began to grow into an immense and real person. The onlooker then watched the twisting lizard grow larger and larger and change into a magnificent silver stallion with golden tail and mane, so powerful that the earth shook as it stamped and whinneyed. The stallion nosed the new-made man who had fallen down in tearful gladness at the feet of the Spirit, and then man and stallion shot away toward the mountains. As they went the earth itself sang a song of vast gladness. They were last seen pushing up the steeps and vanishing into glorious brightness.

Now the onlooker's guide showed him a great procession coming out from the mountains, first bright Spirits dancing and scattering flowers, followed by shapes of boys and girls singing with a glory indescribable, and between them musicians, and then gigantic Angels all making merry. The procession marched to celebrate the honor of Sarah Smith of Golders Green, a woman quite unknown on earth but recognized as truly great in this delectable land. The dancing children who loved Sarah Smith also loved their own parents more, because she had treated them as her children. Even dogs and cats were hers also because of loving treatment, her abundance having flowed into them and made them more themselves than they could have ever been without her. "There is joy enough," said the Guide, "in the little finger of a great saint such as yonder lady to waken all the dead things of the universe into life."

But now, as the Lady advanced, the onlooker saw her turning toward a peculiar looking Ghost, a tall bony man shakily unsure of himself, chained to another Ghost no larger than a monkey. Yet strangely the chain was not for the small Ghost but for the tall one and was attached to a collar around his neck. Now the onlooker observed a remarkable thing! Sarah Smith spoke a most affectionate greeting not to the tall man, a former dramatic actor, but rather to the dwarf Ghost, who had in life been her husband. As she bent over to kiss the dwarf, beatific love flowed from her.

Sarah asked her husband's forgiveness for any wrong done him in life, and now the dwarf jerked the chain and the tragic actor made sentimental and theatrical answers.

Sometimes the dwarf and the actor reassured each other, but mostly it was the dwarf who pulled the chain when the actor was to reply to Sarah. The tragedian complained that he had not been more missed by his wife, that she had actually been happy without him. Sarah tried very hard, with glowing love in looks and words, to tell him of her new life in a place where she had no need for love because she was now living in Love. Come with me, she pleaded to the dwarf, and we can begin to love as we ought. Sometimes her words touched some long lost memory in the dwarf and he grew a little toward man's stature and caused the actor to diminish. But finally the tragedian enlarged and the dwarf faded as he was increasingly absorbed in self-pity and the longing to be loved and deeply missed (a habit which he had begun long before in childhood by sulking in the attic, waiting for someone to pity him and pet him). At last, as Sarah continued her appeal to him to let the light of heaven swallow up his wretchedness, the dwarf disappeared totally into the actor and there was no one left to hear her. As she slowly moved away Bright Spirits came to meet her and sang a song of praise in her honor.

These were some of the ghosts which the onlooker saw on his bus trip from the grey city to the land of abundant life. There were others—for instance, the tripper who was eager to return to the lower regions because the journey was, he felt, simply a propaganda effort. He had only come to look around a bit. He had been to China, Egypt and India and found each place only traps for tourists. Even hell he had found a flop and now viewed the glory of the light over the mountains as only another lie such as he had been hearing from childhood. In his view the "management" should do things to suit the public, not always be asking individuals to change.

There was also the bowler-hatted lover of gold; the woman whose constant preoccupation with the memory of her dead son prevented her from truly caring for her living husband and daughter; also the woman who destroyed her husband by her inordinate ambition for him, and many others. Yet only one of the busload of travelers accepted the warmly proffered invitation to life. All the rest chose instead to return to the self-centered unreality of the grey city.

∞

1. In the eighteenth century William Blake had written a poem called *The Marriage of Heaven and Hell*. Lewis's story, on the other hand, endeavors to represent heaven and hell as far removed from each other, with vast differences between them.

2. The main intent of the story is not to suggest a second chance of salvation nor to propound abstract doctrines about heaven and hell (the narrative is actually presented in the form of a dream) but simply to affirm that people go to hell because they choose not to give up *themselves*. It is best summarized in MacDonald's remark: "There are only two kinds of people in the end: those who say to God, 'Thy will be done,' and those to whom God says, in the end, 'Thy will be done.' All that are in Hell, choose it" (IX). Thus it is a story about that constant called the Self which is operative, moment by moment, in every man's life.

3. Interestingly, all but one of the bus-riders are guilty of "respectable" sins such as love of money, cynicism, gossip, overwrought ambition, misguided intellect, self-importance and the substitution of legalistic morality for Christianity. The only traveler who gives himself up to be changed is guilty of the "bad" sin of lust. In next to the last chapter of *Mere Christianity* Lewis reiterates his warning against the respectable sins that may be the worst ones.

4. Going to hell is not represented as a cataclysmic event as it was for Faust when a man was suddenly tricked into helplessness. Nor is it seen as a deliberate and reasoned decision. Rather it is the culmination of a series of "insignificant" daily acts and choices which push one farther and

farther from Reality, until the time comes when, like the dopester, one finds himself so far down the road to destruction that his choice must almost inevitably follow the course of the rut it has hollowed for itself.

5. One of the values of this story is the sharpening of our normally dull and hazy concepts of both hell and heaven. Hell here is seen as ghostly, quarrelsome and eternally drab, but heaven is made so real that in it men appear like ghosts. Even the farthest glimpse of heaven is one of ineluctable glory. Even the vegetation of heaven is too much for hell.

6. But heaven is by no means simply a place of beatitude and passivity. Rather it is where one actively grows up "into a Person". It is a place of diversity of gift, and its watchword is "farther in and higher up," always in the direction of "Deep Heaven" (IX).

7. As usual, Lewis suggests that negative experiences may open one's spiritual eyes as much as positive ones. Thus the murderer thinking of the horror of his deed is brought to repentance.

8. Charles William's concept of heavenly "co-inherence" is illustrated by its opposite in this story, for in hell the people are pictured as constantly moving farther and farther from each other until some are astronomical distances apart.

9. Lewis, as always, denigrates liberalism in religion. His image of the Episcopal Bishop is a personified summary of his many comments on this subject. On the other hand, he confirms his belief in biblical realities such as the Resurrection (V), "crude salvationism" and repentance and becoming "white as snow" (V). Shame, one of the most difficult experiences of our lives to endure, is recommended as healthy. Drink the cup of shame to its dregs, says he, and you will find it nourishing (VIII). Each must submit to death to himself (XI). Christ is "the Bleeding Charity" (IV) and heaven the place not of questions but of answers, of "Eternal Fact" (V), and before God no man has any "rights."

10. George MacDonald, the nineteenth-century writer and theologian who, more than any other, influenced Lewis, is introduced into the story as one of heaven's glorified saints. He is a guide and teacher and instructs the onlooker (Lewis himself) on a broad range of topics. He reminds him, for instance, that even a spiritual man may become so interested in his dogmatics, such as the proof of God's existence, that he loses his real love for God Himself (IX); that beings in the natural universe are good as they look to God and bad as they turn away from him; and the higher and mightier a thing is in the natural order, "the more demonic it will be if it rebels".

11. Lewis always clearly shows the difference between sentimentalized affection and the strong, firm love which is of God. Indeed, he implies that love for God must precede any genuine love for a fellow creature (XII).

12. Of course this book consistently presents a strong case for man's free will. One must consciously make, not postpone, a choice to be Christ's. "This moment contains all moments" (XI).

13. Lewis never presents salvation as an easy or painless matter. In his autobiography he related his own dreadful experience of having to get down on his knees before God and confess his sins and give up himself. In this story the lustful man had first to come to the point of willing to have "the old man" in him destroyed and then accept suffering prior to the great joy which was given him (XI).

14. As usual, Lewis ends his story on a note of great joy. We see Sarah Smith as a nobody on earth but now celebrated as a queen in heaven, and we learn that she is now *in* Love (XIII). She has attained the quiet and permanent ecstasy which also surrounds the Green Lady in *Perelandra*.

V
The Boy Who Went Around the World

The Pilgrim's Regress

As a child John, who lived in Puritania, learned it was against the rules to pull flowers and kill birds. In due time he was taken by his parents to meet the Steward and after a long lecture came away with two conflicting ideas about the Landlord. One was that if you did wrong he would throw you into a Black Hole infested with snakes and scorpions. The other made the Landlord out to be a very loving sort of person. John was greatly puzzled.

But there was one thing about which he had no doubt at all. Once, having wandered his farthest ever down the road near his home, he saw a beautiful woodland full of the very same sort of primroses he had been forbidden to pick. And as he looked it seemed to him that beyond this loveliness in the green woods he glimpsed, far off, a delectable Island in a calm sea and heard far, sweet music and a voice that said "Come," and with all his soul he wanted it. The intensity of his longing made John forget his parents and the Landlord and everything else and when the music faded he wept bitterly.

Soon John grew tall and more than anything else he desired to see again the lovely woodland and vision of the Island. Sometimes he did get glimpses. Then one day he turned his attention not to the Island but simply to the woods, which he searched diligently without success. Tired and hot, he sat down at last, determined that if he could not have the Island he would try to recapture at least the feeling of it. Just then he heard a voice beside him. It was sweet, though not with the sweetness of the other. It was the voice of a naked brown girl who assured him it was she he really wanted. John committed fornication with her there and afterwards came often to the woods to be with her. But as autumn came on John realized one morning that his beautiful forest was really no more than a shabby stand of ordinary trees. He saw the brown girl as hateful and told her she was not what he really wanted. Smiling ironically at him, she told him when he left to take their daughters along, and he noticed little girls, brown like their mother, behind every tree.

Now John tried hard to follow the Landlord's rules but he was continually hindered by the enticing presence of brown girls on every hand. He concluded there was nothing left but to run away and this he did, walking away from his home in the cold and darkness until morning. And as he went on day after day intent on finding his Island, he began to meet people who, hearing his story, were eager to guide him.

The first was Mr. Enlightenment who, discovering that John was from Puritania, first confidently announced that there was no Landlord and that Puritanians still believed in a Landlord only because they were unenlightened about the real world and the discoveries of science. After more of the same sort of information they parted on a hilltop and for awhile the young man went along almost as joyfully as if he had found his Island, relieved that there was no Landlord and no Black Hole and no rules. He felt delightfully free and did just as he pleased and felt no fear.

Then John met Vertue, a young fellow about his own age, and as they walked together, John found that Vertue was doing a steady thirty miles each day along the main route westward, though he had no real destination such as John's Island and, indeed, no special interest in the Landlord. Vertue had made his own rules and kept them faithfully. Going on, they met an attractive young woman who, hearing of John's search, proposed that he come and see her father in Thrill since he had, at times, talked about something like the Island. John turned off the main highway with Media Halfways (for that was her name) and invited Vertue to come along, but he steadfastly refused.

John and Media walked down a lane toward the city. Soon they were arm in arm, and then John was kissing her, a pleasant experience that reminded him of his Island but also of the troublesome brown girls. Media's father assured John that the only place where the Landlord's castle ever existed was inside us, and as he played and sang a strong, noble tune John began to get such a clear picture of his Island that he was ready to step right into the water leading to it. But the moment the music stopped the vision disappeared. John urged Mr. Halfways to sing the same song again and yet again, but the more he did so the less John liked it. He and Media sat closer together on the sofa, and at last Mr. Halfways left them, saying that each had found the Island in the other. and indeed it seemed so to them. But in the midst of their lovemaking Media's tough brother Gus Halfways threw open the door and informed poor John that Media was only another brown girl and her father in the pay of the Brownies. The spell of the music and the bodily charm of Media had been his downfall.

Next day Gus told John that he was simply ensnared by Romanticism and offered to demonstrate for him the true Realism. Gus drove him northwards across the main highway and through the fields to the city of Eschropolis and there John met the Clevers, people who despised everything normal and espoused virility, obscenity and satire and affected to be totally disillusioned. They also made music for John, but he found that it seemed to reduce his Island to nothing more than a plant in a pot. When John expressed the slightest dislike of their music he was declared a prude, attacked viciously and knocked down. At last he managed, barely, to make his escape. Out of danger, John concluded that while Mr. Halfways took you to the brown girls only after awhile, the Clevers carried you there at once. He limped off down the road and after a long while saw a man mending his fence while he smoked a big cigar. He was Mr. Mammon and John learned that the whole of Eschropolis and its environs was his and its people worked for him.

Because Mammon refused to tell him of a place to spend the night or even where to find a crust of bread, John had to make his way in a freezing rain. Finally he came to a valley with great rocks on each side and a mountain that looked alive and like a man's head. As John attempted to go through a narrow pass he was stopped by guards who asked his mission. When he admitted his search for his Island they arrested him for trespassing on country owned by the Spirit of the Age. His captor, he discovered, was Sigismund, the son of Mr. Enlightenment, who referred to his father as old and ignorant. When Sigismund heard of John's Island he informed him that what John had really wanted was only the brown girls and he had invented the Island to conceal his real lust from himself. He told John also that it was only wishful thinking that made John's parents believe in the Landlord. Puzzled but at least partially convinced by this explanation, John was fettered and thrown into a cold, foul-smelling prison where despair fell upon him and he felt he was truly in the Black Hole.

Because John had argued with some of his jailor's ideas, he was taken out, dragged into the shadow of the mountain (which was indeed alive) and brought to trial. In terror John gave himself up for lost. But just then someone arrived who at first appeared to be another prisoner, yet when free of the dark cloak which covered her, John saw to be a tall steel-clad virgin whose name was Reason. She rode up to the mountain called the Spirit of the Age and slew him with her bright sword, whereupon the mountain crumbled into nothing. As they went on together through the unguarded pass, John learned from Reason that her sisters were Philosophy and Theology but that the people of that land had long since stopped listening to them and so were tricked into all sorts of foolish thinking by the Spirit of the Age. Reason reminded John that though Sigismund had explained John's Island as a wish-fulfillment dream it was equally possible that the Spirit of the Age was simply suffering from his own wish-fulfillment desire that the Landlord should not exist. It worked as well one way as the other. Now John suddenly saw how he had been hoodwinked all the way along by an impudent fraud, and as his eyes were opened to this, the last of his chains fell from off his wrists.

After a time John left Reason and went back to the main highway, a road that ran very straight to the west, and again he came upon Vertue, who had been plodding along steadily all this time as one with no Island to attract him and therefore no reason for hurry. All Vertue could say was that he had acquired muscle and lost soft flesh by his efforts. So they proceeded together until, almost without warning, they came upon a vast chasm into which they nearly fell. It spread before them very wide and very deep. Looking across at the farther side, John thought he saw a rich, tree-covered country.

Puzzled by this obstacle in their path, they wondered what to do next. Vertue was sure they could make their way down the steep cliff somehow, at least part of the way, but John said he had no head for dizzy heights. Just then they heard a voice near them. It was that of Mother Kirk, who was sitting quietly on the very edge of the precipice.

She told John and Vertue that they had no chance of getting down and across without her help. She explained that her power came from the Landlord, who was her father-in-law. But why, asked John should the Landlord leave this dangerous chasm to discourage pilgrims? He did not, said Mother Kirk, and proceeded to tell them the story. Once, said she, the Landlord himself took care of the whole land, which was marvellously beautiful. Desiring to share its beauty with others, he chose a young farmer and his wife and set apart an especially fine part of the country for them. There were mountain-apple trees growing wild everywhere which the Landlord at first thought to eradicate, but then he thought it would be a lesson to the young farmers if he left one large mountain-apple tree there and warned them they should never eat any of its strong, delicious fruit.

In due time they made the acquaintance of another land-owner who had once belonged to the Landlord but after a quarrel with him had become a big land-grabber. This evil entrepreneur persuaded the farmers to eat from the wild-apple tree, and they loved the taste so much that they planted lots of other trees of the same sort and even grafted the tree onto all the other plants so that all the edibles in the land had at least a little of the apple taste in them. It was when the farmer's wife had first pulled an apple off the wild-apple tree that an earthquake had split the land and created this awful chasm.

Then Mother Kirk offered to take them down the danger-ous precipice and across the canyon if they wished, pro-vided they would do exactly as she told them. Now Vertue spoke up and said it was against his way of life to put him-self under anyone's rules, for his deepest desire was to be captain of his own soul. And John, convinced that the old woman was insane, also refused her offer. Vertue explained that they must first try to make their own way down, and she agreed that it would not hurt to make the effort.

John and Vertue traveled northward along the canyon wall looking for a place to descend and as they went they reached the Tableland of the Tough-Minded and visited Mr. Sensible, who advised them to be moderate and try to put the pieces of life together but not grow discouraged if they failed. He thought they might satisfy their curiosity by exploring the cliffs on their own side rather than doing any-thing really hazardous. Their stay with Mr. Sensible was short, for they found his food hardly edible and his house almost too cold to sleep in. They travelled farther north, meeting new people and seeing new landscapes, but conditions grew worse and worse, and John disgustedly saw that they had been on a fool's errand ever since leaving the main highway.

Slowly they made their way back toward the main road. As they went poor Vertue found himself ready simply to lie down and die. He had chosen long before to be what he called a free man, and now he saw that to be motivated with the idea of something pleasant ahead would be to accept a bribe and to be motivated by escaping from something dreadful behind would be to give in to a threat. He despised both and had lived wholly on the assumption that the best life is one of making choices and more choices. He could not accept John's Landlord and the Black Hole because they limited his freedom always to be choosing, the thing he was certain that any honest man must cherish above all else. John finally urged Vertue to stop simply plodding onward and to *want* something, an idea which Vertue rejected. In the freezing darkness Vertue sat down on a stone and said he could see no reason ever to get up. Shortly John missed his friend and after calling out and hunting as best he could in the darkness had to give up. When morning came he again searched, and wept in the process, and at last discovered Vertue lying, apparently dead, on the ground. Indeed he was barely alive, and when John tried to communicate with him found him both blind and dumb, the result perhaps of his shock at realizing the futility of his pilgrimage westward.

With John leading his helpless friend they turned southward and as they went along the sun came out for the first time in many days and they saw hedges greening and heard birds singing. They found some turnips to eat, John showing the blind Vertue how to go about it, and afterwards they lay down (for they were very tired and dirty) and went to sleep. When they awakened they walked on southward into increasingly pleasant countryside with ploughed fields and clumps of woodland. They found a spring and when their thirst was satisfied they began to notice primroses, first a few and then many, and hills growing into mountains in the blue distance.

Afterwards they came to an old ivy-covered brick house which John thought to be that of a Steward, and it indeed proved to that of Mr. Broad. There they were invited to tea on the well kept lawn. As they talked John realized that their host was far more genial and urbane than people he and Vertue had met in the north. Because John never forgot his search for his Island, he asked Mr. Broad for information about the way, but he could learn no more from him than the assurance that "the seeking is the finding," also that Mr. Broad felt that Mother Kirk was really too narrow for him. When John could get nothing more than glowing generalities from his inquiries, he pressed on, having been told that Mr. Wisdom's house was not far ahead. As they went on, the valley they were traversing deepened.

They were welcomed by Wisdom, who sat comfortably among his children. He invited them to stay as long as they would, but John was dismayed when he found that Mr. Wisdom would never quite confirm nor deny the Landlord and the Black Hole and the mountains of the east and west. To his surprise, John discovered that their slow descent had brought them near the bottom of the great divide. He naturally wished to cross over the final crevasse but learned there was no bridge. Not believing wholly in anything on the other side, Mr. Wisdom quite logically assumed that there was nothing for the far end of the bridge to rest upon. Wisdom did not so much discourage John's search for his Island as cause him to lie down indolently in the grass and mollify his fear of the Landlord and moderate his gnawing anxiety about the reality of the Island. On the other hand, Vertue concluded from Mr. Wisdom's lengthy discussions almost the opposite and decided that his proper course was toward fasting and self-torture. Concluding that even friendship is an evil, he forbade John to accompany him when he left.

John followed Vertue at a distance as their valley grew narrower and the sides steeper. Finally each found himself walking along a narrow shelf about half way down the steep side of the grand canyon with great cliffs above and below. When Vertue came to a buttress which totally blocked this shelf he immediately began to scramble up the cliff. Fearing to follow, John sat down, thought matters over and decided to rest a little and go back the way he had come. Then John saw a Man coming down where Vertue had ascended. He offered to help John who, however, insisted that heights made him dizzy. The Man declared he must climb up now or never. He took John's hand and led him, panting and breathless to a narrow ledge, where he left him. Now poor John feared to go either forward or backward. In desperation he tried to apply Mr. Wisdom's philosophy to the situation, but instead soon found himself looking upward and calling loudly for help. Hardly had he ceased when a new terror struck him. He told himself that the Man who helped him was a ghost and he had been praying and was again in bondage to the rules and the slavery and the Black Hole.

As darkness descended John was terrified at the thought of spending the night in such a place. But now the Man appeared again and gave John bread and informed him that a few feet ahead he would find shelter and also a spring in the rock face. Next morning John's first waking thought was terror. He realized that he was totally hemmed in by a Landlord who filled every cranny of the universe. He was a prisoner who should never again be free, never again independent, never again his own man. Nothing was left for him but that one little path along the cliff ahead. So all day, hardly daring to look down, he walked the ledge. As he meditated it dawned on him that the return of the Land-

lord had simply eliminated his Island. A person had replaced a place. But now it also occurred to him that all along
the Landlord must have been quite different from the one
he had imagined.

In a cave in the precipice John now came upon a hermit
whose name was History. To John's surprise, the Hermit
knew all of the country over which John had traveled and
had no very high opinion of it. John learned, to his surprise, that his Island, or some similar image, appeared at
some point to the great majority of men and that such
images came directly from the Landlord. You are here now,
said the Hermit, because the Landlord drew you to himself
by means of that image of beauty. He urged John to go
forward and find Vertue so that they might travel together
again and find help from Mother Kirk.

That night John dreamed that Contemplation came and
led him across the chasm and up the other side and over the
sea and finally over fields and up to high walls and vast
gates and John realized with horror that he was back in his
own eastern mountains and the Landlord's country and the
Black Hole. He tried in his dream to withdraw his hand
from that of Contemplation, but he could not. When he
awakened he determined to escape and went out of the
Hermit's cave and in black darkness, crashing thunder and
brilliant lightning he crawled back along the cliff, his mind
filled with thought of death and scorpions in the Black Hole.
But there Reason, fully armed, met him and sternly ordered
him in the other direction. Poor John, fearful of falling,
managed to turn himself around and crawl back to the cave.

And now came Death and sternly offered John the choice
of jumping or being thrown downwards. John fearfully
agreed to jump, and Death said, "Then I am your servant
and no more your master." John looked down and saw far
below him many dark figures and in their midst a glimmer
of water and near this water someone standing alone. He
felt somehow that he was being waited for. He started down

the cliff and noticed it was no longer as sheer and smooth as he had thought. He managed to get footholds here and there and gradually made his way down to the very floor of the canyon. There he saw a great semicircle of water against high cliffs of the far side and a great company of people, among them Vertue, with their eyes all turned to Mother Kirk.

"I have come to give myself up," said John to Mother Kirk. She welcomed him and explained how she might have saved him much time and disappointment if he had given in sooner. When John asked what he must do, she ordered him to take off his rags and dive into the water. When he said he had never learned to dive Mother Kirk told him it was a ceasing rather than a doing, and Vertue added that John only needed to abandon self-preservation altogether. Actually John had few clothes left, only rags covered with blood and grime acquired in his long journey from Puritania. As he stood hesitating on the edge of the pool, the wraiths of many came up to him from the crowd—old Enlightenment, Media Halfways, Sigismund, Sensible, Broad and others and each advised him to ignore Mother Kirk's orders. But at last, after Vertue had dived in, John managed his own rather clumsy dive.

After a long swim through the deep water under the mountains John and Vertue came up into a land of green forests and rustling leaves and singing birds and were received by a great company of pilgrims who had themselves gone down through the water. Going westward along the banks of a beautiful river, they all wound their way among highlands and lowlands and finally reached the white beaches of the sea at the western end of the world. There in the morning stillness John looked and saw his beloved Island and smelled the sweet odor of it. But now humility made him see it quite differently than before; so different was it that had he first seen it thus he would not have sought it at all.

John and Vertue were now given a Guide to lead them back the way they had come, yet now with new eyes to see. The very first thing he had them do was look again at the Island and notice the shape of its mountains and a dimly perceptible castle on their topmost peak. At first it was with a sinking heart that John recognized the contour of his own eastern mountains and was told by the Guide that he had come clear around the world and that his Island was the very mountain of his childhood memory.

And now beginning at the top of the great divide their Guide led them back over the road they had come, but they found it different country. Their road was now very long and very narrow, with high mountains covered with snow on their left and swamps and jungle on their right. As they went their Guide explained their mistakes on the previous trip. John learned that the Landlord had indeed made the Black Hole but only to provide a final boundary for evil which had begun to spread long before from the taste of mountain-apples. Sometimes they were tempted by some old figure along the way, but now they could clearly see all realities and so won victories rather than suffered defeats. And finally, after meeting and vanquishing both the icy northern Dragon and the flaming Dragon of the south, John and Vertue went on their journey laughing and singing, and they even met a fiddler who played them jigs to dance to.

Now at last they arrived back in Puritania and there saw an abandoned cottage which John recognized as his old home. His father and mother had already crossed the stream. John realized that there was much he now wished he might have said to them. Then their Guide explained how that very night they would also be crossing the stream into the other country. As twilight came on, Vertue and John walked down to the brook singing. There they passed over it, and their Guide sang of the way in which love and sorrow and light and death were all transformed into everlasting joy and song by the Landlord.

∞

Rather late in his life Lewis published an autobiography covering his first thirty years. But much earlier he had written *The Pilgrim's Regress*, which is really an autobiography in narrative form. The title immediately suggests John Bunyan's famous allegory, and indeed there are many parallels, the main one being its description of the events in a journey from sin to salvation. This was Lewis's first Christian book, written at a time when he was deep in scholarly pursuits at Magdalen College, Oxford. In later years he made apology for some of the abstruse elements in the book and added headings that are helpful to a clear understanding. One may profitably read *Surprised by Joy* and *The Pilgrim's Regress* (and perhaps also *The Pilgrim's Progress*) as companion accounts.

1. This is Lewis's story but it is, in terms of the longing to find the source of vision, everyman's, and in terms of fulfillment, the Christian's. All of us know at least some of John's eagerness to gain the goal of true and permanent satisfaction and all have had at least some of John's fruitless wanderings and excursions into the "hard" experiences and philosophies to the north of the main road and also among the "soft" ones to the south. There are also thousands who, like phlegmatic Vertue, plod on stoically down the main road as unwitting as both he and John of the real end to be reached.

2. The story is a veritable catalog of the secularist practices and philosophies of our century, particularly of the thirties when the book was written. In Bunyan's narrative the pilgrim, having some knowledge of the Christian way, is at least aware of his general direction. In Lewis's story both John and Vertue are biblically ignorant and hence "regress," yet still, through persistence, eventually reach the joyful destination.

3. The Landlord, of course, is God and the Steward the local clergyman. John, like others, is completely puzzled

as to how the Landlord can be both a stern legalist and judge and at the same time the fulfillment of his heart-longing for joy. The first Psalm speaks of delight in the law of the Lord, but John had yet to learn of such a combination.

4. Perhaps no more consummate image exists anywhere of the results of the Fall of Man than the long, deep canyon caused by an earthquake on the occasion of man's first sin.

5. The story of the farmer and his wife (Book 5, II) is equally memorable in Lewis's showing, first, of the glories of Eden and God's good gifts to man, including that of free will, and of the one mountain-apple tree to be avoided, of the land-grabber enemy who comes in, the violation of the ban, and, most meaningful of all, the account of how, once mountain-apples were tasted the farmer and his wife could not get enough of them and, by grafting, infected not only other trees but all the varied vegetation of the country. "You have never tasted anything that was quite free from it," said Mother Kirk to John. The Scripture, says St. Paul, "declares that the whole world is a prisoner of sin." (Galatians 3:22, NIV) Thus it is that those who would be saved from the ubiquity of sin must make their way clear down the precipice to the canyon's bottom and cross over.

6. In the revised edition of the story, Lewis takes care to make it clear that Mother Kirk (the Church) is no more than the agent of the Landlord and fully subject to him (Preface). "The book is concerned solely with Christianity as against unbelief," he added.

7. The story takes on special Christian meaning with John's and Vertue's final visit to the grand canyon. In *Surprised by Joy* Lewis tells how, after years of atheism and resistance to the calling of God, he was finally forced to get down on his knees at his bedside at Magdalen College and confess that God was God. The difficulty and excruciating depth of that experience is depicted in powerful detail (141ff) when John found himself clinging to a narrow ledge along the canyon wall. Suffering from a real fear of

"heights" (note the double meaning), he felt unable to go either forward or backward. Finally, in his desperation, he found himself praying. Then "a Man" came to give him food. It was there also that the hermit History interpreted at length the different aspects of the country John had traversed and opened John's eyes to their real nature. Reason and Contemplation also conversed with him. Finally Death came to John and simply ordered him downward, as it were, into a grave, telling him of another fearful descent by no other than the Landlord's own Son. "The cure of death," said Death, "is dying." (Book 9, III) The voice of God spoke similarly to Queen Orual saying, "Die before you die. There is no chance after." (*Till We Have Faces*, Part 2, II) In both cases Lewis means that death to the self and to sin precedes new life in Christ, facts made abundantly clear by a writer such as St. Paul.

8. When John, seeming to have no alternative, fearfully begins his descent to the bottom of the canyon, he finds the way far less dizzy and hazardous than he had expected. In several places Lewis clearly identifies the first token move toward godly obedience and its resultant heavenly encouragement. As he walked in the dewy morning grass with Aslan, Edmund the traitor became the Lion's joyful follower and staunch defender. (*The Lion, the Witch and the Wardrobe*, XIII) When Mark Studdock finally became convinced of the evil of Belbury and resolved if necessary to die for right things, a clear direction immediately appeared to him and he felt a new freedom and joy. (*That Hideous Strength*, XV, 4)

9. How complete is John's final confession, "I have come to give myself up" (Book 9, IV). Mother Kirk's answer is for him to strip off his dirty rags. "All our righteousnesses are as filthy rags," (Isaiah 64:6) and John's were indeed plastered with blood and grime. Even a piece of his skin came off with the cloth. He needed the kind of radical renewal that Aslan gave, not without pain, to Eustace in *The Voyage of the Dawn*

Treader, also the painful renewal experienced of the lustful man in *The Great Divorce*.

10. But in all these cases the pain was followed by great joy. At last John, having gone through the water of baptism, experienced, in the silence of early morning light, a view of his long-sought Island and smelled the enchanting odor of its orchards (Book 9, V). But now the Island as such became absorbed in a truer image, that of the Landlord himself, yet a totally different Landlord from the one John had earlier supposed. He found that his longing, intense and delectable, was not for brown girls and Media Halfways and Zeitgeistism, nor for either a hard or soft philosophy, but from the first had been a longing for the Lord God, the essence of what theologians call "universal grace."

11. Lewis clearly teaches that Christian eyes see a different world from non-Christian ones. John and Vertue found their road back to Puritania long and narrow, with cold and dangerous mountains on one side and fetid swamps and jungles on the other. Christ said, " ... strait is the gate, and narrow the way, which leadeth unto life." (Matthew 7:14) They clearly realized the futility of John's tangential excursions away from the road and Vertue's stolid plodding with no real end in view.

12. Again Lewis places a high value on Reason. This "sun-bright virgin clad in complete steel" and carrying a naked sword, made a quick end of the Spirit of the Age (Book 3, IX). Later she came to John on the narrow canyon path and summarily ordered him to turn and go in the right direction (Book 9, IV). The fact that Lewis placed the house of Wisdom near the level of the canyon suggests that he found it more nearly palatable than others which John and Vertue had met. In the first edition of *The Pilgrim's Regress* Lewis had identified Wisdom's dogma as Philosophical Idealism, actually the final phase of belief Lewis went through before he became a Christian. There he also explained Wisdom's views as ones in which, at last, John

found "a rational account both of his nameless Desire and of his moral obligations." We learn, however, that Wisdom's position has been much tainted with many of the dogmas and practices which John had been encountering all the way from Mr. Halfways (Book 7, X) as well as something from Mother Kirk. We learn also that the valley in which Wisdom's house was located had once been called the Valley of Humiliation, but was no longer (Book 7, VIII).

13. The following translations and transliterations of names and phrases are intended to help make the meaning of *The Pilgrim's Regress* more accessible:

"Ichabod" (Book 1, V; 2, VI): "The glory has departed." (I Samuel 4:21)

"Que[m] Quaeritis in Sepulchro? Non est Hic." (Book 1, VI): "Whom do you seek in the tomb? He is not here." (Luke 24:5-6)

"Dixit Insipiens" (Book 2, I): "The fool said . . ." (Psalms 14:2)

"Eschropolis" (Book 3, I): A shameful city.

"Archtype and Ectype" (Book 4, II; 8, X): Original and copy.

"Esse/est/Percipi" (Book 4, III): "To be is to be perceived." It seems to mean, "*Really to be* means to be perceived or understood." Note the negative way in which Reason puts the case to John, "Is it surprising that things should look strange if you see them as they are not?" and "A man cut open is, so far, not a man."

"Peccatum Adae" (Book 5, II; 9, IV): "The sin of Adam." (Romans 5:12-21)

"Regum aequabit opes animis" (Book 5, IV): "We are what our thoughts make us."

"Omnes edodem cogimur" and "quo dives Tullus et Ancus" (Book 5, IV): "We are all driven towards the same end, death, where are rich Tullus and Ancus."

"Nullius Addictus" (Book 5, IV): "I am not bound over to swear allegiance to any master: where the wind carries me,

I put into port and make myself at home." (From Horace.)

"J'aime le jeu . . . ." (Book 5, IV): "I love entertainment, love, books, music, the city and country—everything!"

"Haud equidem invideo" (Book 5, IV): "I am by no means envious."

"Caelum non animum mutamus" (Book 5, IV): "We change our climate, not our soul."

"Et ego in Arcadia!" (Book 5, IV): Loosely, "I, too, am an idealist."

μονόχρονος ἡδονή (Book 5, IV): "momentary pleasure"

"Eadem sunt omni semper" (Book 5, IV): "Everything remains always the same."

"Auream quis . . ." (Book 5, IV): "Whoso cherishes the golden mean, safely avoids the foulness of an ill-kept house." (From Horace.)

"Do manus!" (Book 5, IV): "I give up, surrender."

"Dapibus mensas onerabat inemptis" (Book 5, V): This is a continuation of the "Regum" passage in the previous chapter. The allusion is to an old Corsican who had very poor land but managed to plant a few seeds of herbs and flowers and make them grow and so "matched the wealth of kings by his spirit" and "loaded his table with unbought dainties."

'Αθάνατους μὲν πρῶτα θεούς νόμῳ ὡς διάκειται—Τιμα (Book 5, V): "First of all, honor the immortal gods as the law ordains."

"Cras ingens iterabimus" (Book 5, V): "Tomorrow we shall set out once more upon the boundless sea."

"Pellite cras ingens tum-tum νόμῳ ὡς διάκειται" (Book 5, V): Mostly meaningless. A hazard at translation might result in "Drive out the great tomorrow tum-tum as the law demands."

Note: We can take all these remarks by Mr. Sensible (Book 5, IX-VII) with a large grain of salt. He is obviously a scatterbrain attempting to bolster his essential ignorance with supposed quotations from classical authors.

"Virtutes paganorum splendida vitia" (Book 6, II): "The virtues of the pagans are splendid vices."

"Epichaerecacia" and "Euphuia" (Book 6, II): The names of Mr. Enlightenment's wives, the first a malicious woman, one who "joyed over her neighbor's misfortune," the second with a pleasant disposition.

"Marxomanni" (Book 6, VI): Probably "Followers of Marx."

"Nycteris" (Book 7, VIII): "Bat"

"Evangelium eternum" (Book 7, XII): "The everlasting gospel"

"Clopinel in Medium Aevum" (Book 8, X): Clopinel was Jean de Meun of the thirteenth century, i.e., "Medium Aevum" or Middle Ages. In this passage Lewis is speaking of the manner in which God continues through the generations to give people a longing such as John's for his Island. Like John, they misunderstand and counteract and even ridicule, yet the longing continues to manifest itself not through those who ridicule but perhaps through "the stupidest tenant." (Book 8, IX).

"Securus Te Projice" (Book 9, IV): "Cast yourself down untroubled."

"Nella sua Voluntade" (Book 9, VI): "In His will is our peace." (From Dante.)

"Slikisteinsauga" (Book 9, VI): "Holy Spirit" or "Guardian Angel."

"Serpens nisi serpentem comederit" (Book 10, VIII): "A serpent unless he has eaten a serpent" (Cf. *The Voyage of the Dawn Treader*, (V)

"Resurgam and Io Paean . . . !" (Book 10, X): "I shall rise again and shout for joy, Io Paean, Io Paean."

VI
Getting A Face
Two Ways

That Hideous Strength

Jane and Mark

Jane and Mark Studdock, married in church six months earlier but not back again, are intelligent and sophisticated. She is completing her work for a doctorate in literature and he is a junior Fellow in sociology at Bracton College. They like to be liked and revel in the cozy exclusiveness of inner circles. Neither profane nor cruel, yet more inwardly crabbed than they imagine, they simply wish to get ahead and their lives are aimed steadily upward without particular moral direction.

Their brief marriage has not altogether satisfied either of them, especially Jane, who sees Mark immersing himself in college politics while she too often sits listless at home. As their plans call for no children, Jane is quite free to pursue her literary scholarship, yet somehow the ambition has diminished, part of it perhaps owing to the disappearing joys of courtship and the increasing marital tilts and resentments between them. Their natural prospects for a generous and cheerful home life grow steadily more meager.

And yet a generous and cheerful home they are destined to have, but only as the climax to courses of action which neither of them could have anticipated.

Mark is carried to the National Institute for Co-ordinated Experiments (N.I.C.E.) at Belbury in a handsome automobile that races out of Edgestow and roars down country roads daring anything to interfere, a car driven by Feverstone, a man Mark sees, a bit nervously to be sure, as Somebody destined for Big Things. And Mark, who might have gone on for years being a nobody at little Bracton, now harbors deep within him an ambition for sudden prominence and perhaps fame. He knows only vaguely of Belbury's publicly announced intentions to do great things for England by the application of scientific methods to the whole of life, but he has no idea of its real intention to destroy on a cosmic scale and recreate in the image of hell.

At the very time Mark is rushing to Belbury one might notice Jane, in another direction, sitting in a little train slowly chugging up from Edgestow to the village of St. Anne's. She has reluctantly agreed to see friends there in hopes of relief from strange dreams that, to her astonishment, seem to come true. Looking out the window of her climbing train one might see the autumn sunlight on haystacks, and horses standing meditatively in open fields, and rabbits with inquisitive ears up, while on the train were country people who spoke amiably to each other with no trace of the insane rush Mark was then both enjoying and suffering.

Perhaps there is nowhere else in Lewis a better image of two ways of life, one busy, intent, nervous, ruthless and the other quiet, observant, acceptive and generous. One indeed, we finally note, leads Mark almost to Satanism, while the other guides Jane to total joy.

None of the loveliness of that countryside just then impressed Jane, unless by some subtlety unknown to her, and neither did the growing green vegetables, the flowers and the mossy paths within the stone walls of St. Anne's. Even as she went into the great quiet house she felt rebellious. But there, still skeptical but deeply hoping for release from her prophetic dreams, she told her story to Miss Ironwood, the physician. From her she learned, to her horror, that this was not an illness and tht her dreams neither could nor should be avoided. They were indeed a gift, either for good or ill. Jane left St. Anne's puzzled and upset and with a definite resolve never to return. Yet somehow, without any conscious knowledge of it, Jane had imperceptibly begun to take on a "face."

Now evil days were beginning for the little city of Edgestow. The first Jane knew of them was during an overnight visit from Mrs. Dimble, wife of a distinguished Professor at Bracton and friend to Jane and Mark. When bedtime came, Mother Dimble, to Jane's embarrassment, got down beside her bed for her evening prayer. Jane said nothing, but a bit of a totally strange world quietly entered her. Talk of most anything else under the sun would not have bothered Jane, but genuine devotion to God created in her only an embarrassed silence.

Mark was offered a new position at Belbury which left Jane with long stretches of quiet at home. She was glad when Camilla Denniston, a charming woman about Jane's own age, with an equally attractive husband, invited her to a picnic with them. As they ate they talked of St. Anne's, which was natural because the Dennistons belonged there. Having confessed in the conversation that still another dream of hers had come true, Jane was urged to join St. Anne's. But when they added that the Pendragon, the head of St. Anne's, would require Jane to come in freely or not at all, her natural antagonism to being "drawn in" was accentuated. As they talked, Jane pictured St. Anne's as a place of some bizarre ritual dominated by men and particularly by a man such as this Pendragon, whose name was Ransom. Though Jane refused to have any part of St. Anne's, she consented to inform the Dennistons of any new dreams. But on this outing she had spent some hours with people of gentleness, good sense, quiet spirits and elemental honesty, and she was unknowingly changed.

Jane's next dream, that of a Belbury man being slain, shocked her so much that now for the first time she longed to be with people of the sort she met at St. Anne's. Her earlier intention always to be "her own" had quietly shifted because of her association with Mrs. Dimble and the Dennistons. Once again Jane boarded the little train for St. Anne's but now with eyes open to the gentle countryside as her train climbed up through the fog, into the bright warm sunshine and blue sky. Unlike her earlier trip during which Jane had been perplexed about how to act when she arrived, this time she sat quietly. Being with good people, Jane was becoming better herself.

Among the people of St. Anne's Jane discovered great concern over her last dream and an eager desire for her to see the mysterious Pendragon. In all the talk about him there had been a deference far above mere respect, and again Jane envisioned a male-dominated community and a man elevated to a point unacceptable in her scheme for equality of the sexes. It was an image that both her personal wishes and her education rebelled against.

Finally consenting to see him, Jane was taken up stairways and through halls in which the warm autumn sunlight made patterns on the soft carpets. She had no idea that she was entering the greatest experience of her life, and as she went she steeled herself against getting involved and becoming one more admirer of this Head, whoever he might be. What she found was a man apparently not as old as herself, if his fine skin and fresh countenance were considered, yet full-bearded and with strong hands and shoulders and with a tranquil bearing about him gained from visits into Deep Heaven and agelessness—the appointed Pendragon of Earth, the Fisher-King, the Ransomer of a planet which might have otherwise become another fallen world.

The very first glance after the door opened unmade her whole existence. When Jane looked at him she now knew the meaning of the word King as a ruler both powerful and merciful. In Ransom's presence all sorts of images rushed through her consciousness. His welcoming voice gave her the impression of sunlight and gold. She felt her old sophistication and resentment flow out of her and some sort of cleansing take place. In some fashion she now understood honesty and straightforwardness. She was gaining a true face.

When it looked as if Jane might be prohibited from St. Anne's because Mark was at Belbury, she begged now to come. As the Pendragon inquired about the relationship between her and Mark she found a strange new way of thinking taking possession of her. The good things in this man before her reminded her of good things in Mark that she had overlooked. She even began to understand how obedience was an avenue leading not to shameful subjection but rather to inner peace. Marriage, she now understood, was to be a dance in which both loved and both were obedient in their order. The interview ended with Jane feeling emptied and small and weak. It had been so overwhelming that she was relieved when the Pendragon dismissed her.

She walked out experiencing an entirely new mode of thought. Descending into Edgestow, she looked out the train window and everything gave her joy—sunlight on trees and fields and cattle and rabbits and inside the carriage the charm of a wrinkled old man who sat next her. She suddenly recalled the glory of music and made plans to listen to some at home. She experienced beauty, even her own beauty, and she wanted Mark to possess her beauty.

But instead of music and poetry, Jane was next to suffer abject terror at the hands of the Belbury police, for Belbury had now discovered Jane's prophetic ability and intended to make their own diabolical use of it. Through a momentary distraction Jane managed to escape, after suffering physical torture and now knowing Belbury as a menace. She hurried back to St. Anne's. Her wounds were dressed and she was put to bed. Next morning she awakened to a feeling of blessedness and the great hope that she might be allowed to remain. She had a delicious day in bed reading books that, in her sophistication, she would earlier have scorned. That day Jane made the acquaintance of Mr. Bultitude, the beloved bear at St. Anne's, and one of various animals and birds dwelling there.

Now joyful in the presence of Ransom, she realized that her prescient dreams, horrible as they were, might help to destroy Belbury and release Mark. She learned of Ransom's visits to Malacandra and Perelandra and the peoples he had found on those planets, including eldils, very much like angels, and how Belbury, and indeed the whole earth, was under the domination of evil eldils. She learned that on one planetary trip Ransom had fought and slain the body of a devil-possessed man who had managed to inflict on Ransom a permanent wound in the heel. In the same house with the Pendragon and among friends such as the Dennistons and Dimbles and even Jane's own charwoman Mrs. Maggs, and despite the dangers to Mark and to the world, Jane was now happier than she could imagine. The old life of pride and selfishness had quietly disappeared and for the first time she felt totally alive. Old things had passed away and all things were in process of becoming new.

She concluded that nothing less than God could have opened such horizons to her. Long before, she had told the Pendragon that though she knew nothing of God she would put herself under the good auspices of St. Anne's. Overwhelmed by new facts and feelings pouring into her, Jane went out into the lovely garden of St. Anne's to meditate. There it occurred to her that the people of St. Anne's never talked about religion. They talked about God. How strange that was to her. A Person, not an exhalation, not a ghost. Suddenly, just as Jane was passing the gooseberry bushes, a change came over her, quietly but inexorably. Jane's old ways fell off her and a new way—no, a Person—filled up her life to overflowing. An unspeakable quietness and joy told her that her face, her being, was made wholly new.

Mark was driven pell-mell to Belbury not knowing that already he and Bracton College had been hoodwinked. In contrast to Jane's original wish not to get involved at St. Anne's, Mark was eager to climb right into the inner circle at Belbury. He was proud enough to suppose himself an intellectual and a realist with no small measure of cynicism for the normal and the ordinary. Not without a conscience, and yet never having given much thought to ethics as such, Mark began quietly, as Jane after a different fashion had done at St. Anne's, to take on the coloring of his environment. Used to the jargon of sociology, he fell into imitating the vacuous talk of Wither, the Director. Had he used his boasted intelligence he might have been warned by the very names of the Belbury leaders—Wither and Frost and Steel and Stone. He did occasionally complain at Belbury, especially about his inability to learn what was his real work there. He even threatened to leave, but in fact he finally obeyed what he was told. Whatever fragments of genuineness Mark had were slowly being drained from him. He was merely embarrassed, not morally horrified, at meeting an apostate preacher named Straik, highly placed in the organization, who vigorously declared that Belbury was to bring in the kingdom of God not by love but by lies and, when necessary, by murder. Mark was ordered to write lying newspaper articles that would result in rioting and confusion, and the time came when, reading his articles in print, he could smile at his own cleverness. Thus he acquired more and more of Belbury's dark ways.

And now he made a truly terrifying discovery. As part of Belbury's intention to make him a member of the most inner circle of all, his initiation began and he was led into a dimly lighted room smelling of chemicals where he found a human head being kept "alive," by means of tubes and wires attached to dials. Many at Belbury viewed this as nothing more than a scientific experiment. Wither and Frost, however, had their own aim, which was to eliminate death. They wished to make man immortal—his own God. Furthermore these men had more than natural aid in their plans. They had the aid of bent eldils, even of Satan himself. And now Mark discovered that he had been selected to become a third in a devil-possessed triumvirate.

Since their marriage, Mark had given Jane a minimum of thought. Now in her absence he began to see her clearly. His superiors, having learned of Jane's prophetic gifts and wishing to make use of them, ordered Mark to bring her to Belbury. But Mark was determined to prevent this. He had enough good sense left to know that Jane would feel totally out of place in the decadent atmosphere of Belbury. He could not imagine Jane in the presence of "Fairy" Hardcastle, the fat, frowsy, coarse, cigar-smoking female chief of N.I.C.E. police, a bully and ready to commit murder as need be. Now remembering many of Jane's good qualities that he had taken for granted, Mark grew to hate Belbury and to have no greater hope than escape. When, finally, he did escape and hurry home, eager to see Jane, he found her missing. He called on Dr. Dimble and learned of Jane's torture by the sadist Hardcastle, also that she was hidden away—hidden indeed from her own husband and the beastly Belbury.

All of Mark's blustering and disclaimers fell away from him as he talked with this good man. He saw why Dr. Dimble should hate Belbury with a pure hatred, for Dimble knew, to Mark's surprise, all about the false newspaper articles, the severed head and even about the murder of Hingest, a Belbury scientist who had rebelled. Though disgusted with Mark, Dimble felt sorry for him and offered to try to help him. Full of fears, false self assurances and excuses, Mark left Dimble and went to his college. Just as he reached it the police from Belbury arrested him for the murder of Hingest.

This false charge was Belbury's way of forcing Mark to produce Jane. Refusing, he was imprisoned. Concluding now that he would surely be killed, he began for the first time to consider death and even heaven and immortality. He looked at his hands and realized they would perhaps soon be dead hands on a dead body. In memory he saw all his wrong decisions and actions as one immense deviation from the normal and the decent. Beginning with little smirks and nods of agreement to wrong things, he had sunk deeper not simply into folly but into an organization intent on abolishing mankind in the image of God. He saw all the clues he had missed right at the beginning and how he had been taken in time after time, taken in indeed since boyhood. Along with a good deal of self-pity, his thoughts turned to such people as the Dimbles and Dennistons and their tranquil, yet joyful confidence. And again he thought warmly of Jane and began to see in her much that he had overlooked. He knew now that Belbury was his unalterable enemy and if necessary he must die opposing it.

And now began the concluding efforts of Wither and Frost to bring Mark to subjection to the Macrobes, or bent eldils of earth under the control of Satan. As Mark learned of the enormous scope of this scheme and its devilish objective, he began at last to think clearly of right and wrong, but hardly had his conscience cleared before he began to commend himself as a sort of hero and a vast black sucking sensation of lust and craving took possession of him. It was the last mighty effort of the Macrobes, right there in his cell, to destroy him. When he began to recover he realized the contrast between their vast strength and his own feeble will to resist. Humbled, he began to long for people like the Dimbles and Jane. He prayed. He did not really know he was praying, only crying out from his heart for help. Slowly, strangely Mark relaxed and felt a kind of peace. Some new order of things was taking place in him there in his prison. Very tired, he fell peacefully asleep.

Now Frost came to Mark's cell and began a long philosophic effort to prove that man must needs cooperate with creative evolution simply because that process was obviously occurring. Good, he told Mark, is constantly being generated by this evolutionary force and hence all external standards of value are the result largely of emotion rather than any real observation of the facts. Mark retorted that by such a standard Belbury's intentions to destroy all organic life was a "good" thing. Frost readily agreed. Then it dawned on poor Mark that actually he had based his whole life on assumptions as pragmatic and cold as those at Belbury. He had believed in physical facts as "real" and spiritual or emotional ones as merely subjective. He had erased truly human meanings in favor of "real facts." The higher had simply been swallowed by the lower. He was overcome by the dawning of clean new horizons. And now with all his strength he rejected everything that Belbury stood for.

Unlike Jane, who came to the light through warmth and love, Mark now began to see that same light through reason. Wither and Frost, not knowing of any change in Mark, commenced a series of exercises intended to destroy in Mark all clearly human reactions and join him to the Macrobes, the very process by which earlier they had themselves become demon-guided. Frost took Mark into a room where an almost lifesized crucifix lay on the floor and ordered him to insult it by stamping on it. Mark noted the illogicality of the atheists at Belbury seeing the crucifix as more than a piece of wood.

In the same moment Mark experienced something else. He looked intently down at the calm, defenseless figure on the cross and felt equally defenseless in the brutal hands of Belbury. Mark still did not believe in Christ, but he remembered that Christ had been crucified by the Belbury kind of people. He was struck by the fact that long ago the Straight had met the Crooked, and here at his feet was the symbol that the straight had often gone down before the crooked. Was that a reason, he asked himself, for him now to be joined to the crooked? Despite Frost's increasing threats, and knowing that refusal probably meant death, Mark flatly refused the desecration. Like Jane at St. Anne's, Mark was in process of acquiring a face.

At that moment serious interruptions began to signify the

end of Belbury and allowed Mark to escape.

At daylight Mark wandered into a little country hotel where he took a bath, had a good breakfast and then went to sleep in front of a bright fire. Hours later when he awakened he noticed there a children's story that he had first started to read as a little boy and then, ashamed and wishing to feel grown-up, had dropped. Now, with the old ways being rapidly washed out of him he enjoyed every word. Seeing himself as little less than a vulgarity to people such as the Dimbles and Dennistons, he now grew in desire to be like them. He had only vague ideas about St. Anne's. What he did know was that the *right* sort of "inner circle" was there and he fervently wished to join Jane, and it.

As he went along he reviewed his attitude toward Jane and deeply resolved to be a proper husband. He saw in Jane the essence of what he thought he wanted to be. He did not know that Jane was herself a new creature with the old pride and resentments washed away. He was unaware that she was now overcome and fulfilled by the predominance of love at St. Anne's and that she had discovered, in this quiet house, the very center of the true England. It was Logres, and the unageing Ransom was the true Pendragon, the real Fisher-King, leader of the remnant that by unearthly grace and quiet dependence could bring about the overthrow of evil men and bent eldils, for circumstances had by now made Belbury a total ruin.

Ransom had assigned Jane and Mark a cottage off the main house at St. Anne's, and now they were able to come together again, each having understood and repented of their shallow, selfish conduct toward the other. Neither yet knew of the changes in the other, and were unaware of the clear overflowing joy awaiting them as renewed husband and wife, Jane now under the wings of Everlasting Love and Mark surely approaching that same blessedness.

∞

Although the setting of this novel is on earth, it is properly the third member of the space trilogy as it describes the blessed invasion of eldils from the heavens and of space-traveler Ransom, now elevated yet still warmly dependent upon powers greater than himself.

The Belbury portion of the story is an anti-utopian work that should be read in connection with Lewis's *The Abolition of Man*, where he speaks of the *Tao* or universal moral order and the dangers emergent when that order is ignored or circumvented. Frost, for instance, one of Belbury's leaders, proclaims that any external or given standard of value is simply preposterous (XIV, 1).

1. By getting a face Lewis means coming to a point of total honesty with one's deepest self, dropping one's habitual masks (some of which may have been carried a lifetime, especially the mask of self-deception).

2. Primarily this novel deals with a series of contrasts in which great evil is the converse of great good, the former identified with the National Institute of Co-ordinated Experiments (N.I.C.E.) at Belbury and the latter with St. Anne's. The evil shows up at different levels, running all the way from a nasty college clique to literal devilishness. As the story proceeds we learn that the head of Belbury is neither Wither nor Frost, nor the actual head of a man being kept alive, but rather powerful demons of fallen earth, and that the human agents, both good and bad, are being acted upon by the supernatural. Belbury consists of circles within circles with the topmost represented by Wither and Frost who, like Weston in *Perelandra*, are demon-possessed, a condition that has made Wither into "a shapeless ruin" and Frost into a "hard, bright, little needle" (XIV, 1) and both with purposes fully as devilish as that of the Un-man. Like the Un-man they hate the disgrace of death and decay, seeing—or at least preferring to see—no connection between them and the Fall of Man and intent on giving man their own brand of everlasting life.

3. Images of good, however, are constantly contrasted

with those of evil. Having been twice into the glory of the heavens and having saved Perelandra from the fate of "man's first disobedience," [in the process receiving the incurable wound in his flesh] Ransom is now no longer subject to ageing and death and is the Fisher-King and Pendragon. Lewis, in fact, calls Ransom a "Christ figure." His headship at St. Anne's is marked by quietness and love, yet the time comes when he has to inform his people that, contrary to their beliefs, they have come together under one roof not through any plan of his but only through the wisdom of his "Masters," the planetary Oyeresu (or angels) who are in their turn the servants of Maleldil.

How dependent St. Anne's is on a higher leadership is clearly shown by Ransom's refusal to let MacPhee, the skeptic and non-Christian at St. Anne's, play any major part in the final struggle against Belbury, because, as Ransom tells him, these others are "heavily protected as you are not" (X, 4). To MacPhee's insistence that, in this obvious crisis for mankind, direct and immediate action is desperately required (such as a national organization and maybe the formation of a party in the House of Commons) Ransom again shows his quiet dependence upon orders from the angelic company he has learned to trust. And this trust is rewarded not only with victory over Belbury but with the coming to earth of all the planctary angels with their supernal strength and glory. One familar with Acts 2 may find a number of parallels between the coming of the Oyeresu and the glorious visitation of the Holy Spirit at Pentecost.

4. MacPhee, St. Anne's skeptic, prides himself on his powers of logic and is inclined to raise doubts about anything but what he calls "veridical" proof. Lewis presents him as a necessary and loved member of St. Anne's and does so perhaps because Lewis himself likes the idea of an *advocatus diaboli*. (He himself frequently became such an advocate, as in the opening of *The Problem of Pain* where he

begins by stating the case for atheism as clearly as perhaps it has ever been stated in brief, only thereafter to demolish it.) If a Biblical parallel with MacPhee were needed, one might cite the dialectic of the Book of Job.

5. It is the "weak" (I Corinthians 1:27) St. Anne's with its trust in God, and freedom, that overcomes the complex, organized activism of Belbury. Yet one always notes that St. Anne's is informed and ready for action when the time comes, not sitting idly and eschewing responsibility.

6. Like any other good Christian, Lewis always looks for God in the events of history. Ransom reminds MacPhee that the unbreakable laws of the universe are never violated, not even by miracle, and that his fundamental error is an insufficient awareness of the larger "divine clearness" which is not confined to a few centuries or simply to our little earth (XVI, 4). Even a rascal like Frost acknowledges that "Macrobes," or powers beyond investigation, are always around and believes that the "real causes of all the principal events are quite unknown to historians" (XII, 4). Like Weston, his Macrobes are diabolical, yet in his way he does better than many who declare a belief in God and yet somehow remain essentially unaware of the supernatural. It is interesting that Will and Ariel Durant, after a lifetime of writing history, conclude: "Most history is guessing, and the rest is prejudice." Certainly Christians believe that any history which ignores the real Cause of all things is bound to be at least partially false.

7. A point deserving mention is Belbury's low opinion of nature. Lewis was a lifelong foe of vivisection, a practice inevitable at Belbury. He was also the enemy not of science proper but of "scientism" or the supposition that no problem is beyond the reach of the scientific method, a belief built into the very core of Belbury, at least at all levels below that of the demonized Wither and Frost. At Belbury, Filistrato, in his radical antisepticism, plans to do away with real trees and birds in favor of artificial ones that he can

control, a far cry from both the viewpoint of St. Anne's, where nature was both respected and loved, and from hundreds of Biblical passages in which nature as God's creation is fervently extolled.

Of particular interest is Ransom's remark to Merlin that since his time fifteen hundred years ago, "the soul has gone out of wood and water" (XIII, 5). Lewis, like his friend Owen Barfield, believed that the history of the world is the history of man's separating himself from God on one hand and from nature on the other, a direction derived from man's increasing wish to elevate himself and thus belittle all else. Christians tend to see God as creator in terms of His original activity but fail to recognize that the continued proliferation of trees, shrubs, grass, flowers and vegetables in their own yards is equally miraculous. In fact, a Christian may profitably ask himself precisely when, outside his "religious" activities in church and home, God has an active part in his life.

8. Both Mark and Jane go to places previously unknown to them and both gradually take on the color of their surroundings and learn to speak the language. Mark, for instance, becomes a willing liar in his journalistic writing while Jane in the presence of Ransom, finds even minor hypocrisy impossible (VII, 2). In each of them the symbol of final spiritual awareness is the wish to read childhood stories, a strong echo of our Lord's remark that childlikeness is a mark of the Kingdom of Heaven.

9. Aware of man's bent to sin, Lewis is equally sure of God's ultimate victory. His symbols are Britain versus Logres, where Britain represents man's seemingly inevitable tendency to apostacy and degeneration of spirit, (as manifest at Belbury), while Logres symbolizes in each generation a group fully true to the faith, such as that at St. Anne's (XVII, 4). Lewis believed that if no more than ten per cent of people possessed genuine holiness they would be irresistible and would bring about worldwide salvation in short order.

10. Again Lewis warns the Christian about the likelihood of an attack from Satan following a real Christian experience. One instance is that of Jane just after she has experienced salvation and is promptly beset with devilish appeals (XIV, 6). Mark also, having at last done what his conscience strongly suggested and felt the good consequences, was "sucked and tugged" into heroics, lust and Satanism itself before finally he began to attain some peace (XII, 7). Out of this he began to see his desperate condition clearly and out of it came his first real prayer for help with all its good consequences. Lewis wrote Sheldon Vanauken just after he had become a Christian that he must look out for a counter attack by Satan. "The enemy," he said, "will not see you vanish into God's company without an effort to reclaim you." (*A Severe Mercy*, p. 102)

11. As always, Lewis in this story presents a God who is not "tame." The final judgment on Belbury is shockingly complete. I suspect that he had at least partly in mind II Thessalonians 1:7-8, where we are told that the Lord "shall be revealed from heaven with his mighty angels, in flaming fire taking vengeance on them that know not God." At St. Anne's the coming of the Oyeresu is also overwhelming. Even Ransom, who had been in the heavens and met the great planetary Oyeresu, could barely withstand the onrush of their blessed coming.

12. As in the previous volumes of the space trilogy, Lewis the philologist makes good use of the intimations of the Biblical story of the tower of Babel and of a time when the whole earth was of one language and of men who had to be punished by "confounding" of their speech. (Genesis 11:1, 6-9) Lewis gives us an exciting notion of original speech, that which Adam and Eve may have spoken, when Dimble at Ransom's command speaks "great syllables of words that sounded like *castle*" and are actually part of the "Great Tongue" given by Maleldil (X, 4).

13. Although *That Hideous Strength* contains much hor-

ror, it ends in glory. In this case there is a three-fold joy, the joy of victory over Belbury, the joy of Jane and Mark's reunion and acquisition of true sanity, and the joy of the grand visit to earth of the planetary angels to carry Ransom into the heavens.

VII
Getting A Face
Two Other Ways

Till We Have Faces

Orual and Psyche

Orual and Psyche were daughters of Trom, king of Glome, a barbarian city on the river Shennit with a temple to Ungit, a fertility mother-goddess. The first time Orual laid eyes on her baby sister Psyche she was overcome with unutterable joy, for lovely Psyche seemed to brighten the very atmosphere around her.

As Psyche grew into girlhood she continued to radiate love and beauty, so much so that the Fox, a beloved Greek slave purchased by King Trom to tutor his daughters, confessed that she looked like an "undying spirit."

In those days the two girls liked to visit a hill on the southwest of Glome where they could look down on the city. But on such occasions Psyche always found herself gazing across toward the Grey Mountain on the other side and would startle Orual and the Fox by saying that some day she would be a queen married to the "greatest king of all" and live up there with him in a gold and amber castle. Strangely enough, Orual, deeply as she loved Psyche, felt uneasy at such remarks. Deep down she wanted Psyche always to be her very own and not another's.

Now Glome suffered a succession of bad years. The Shennit dried up and crops were ruined. The priest of Ungit, the goddess of the land (represented by a black stone sitting deep in the shadows in the temple) declared that nothing less than a human sacrifice could bring rain and renewed life. Lots were cast and, to the horror of all at the palace, and particularly of Orual, Psyche was chosen to die. The day came when Psyche, who realized more clearly than the others that one must sometimes die for all, uttered no complaint as she was ceremonially robed, her face was gilded and painted and she was given a sweet, sticky drug to drink. Then all the people followed the king and the priest of Ungit as Psyche was taken on the long journey to the top of the Grey Mountain and there chained to a dead tree, according to the ancient custom, and left to die.

Because Orual had been injured, she remained at the palace in great pain and with a far greater inner hurt because her beautiful and purehearted sister had thus been chosen for torture and death. When Orual was recovered enough she took Bardia, the head of the king's guard, and, supposing Psyche to have been eaten by wild animals, left Glome and climbed the mountainside to pay proper respect to the memory of her sister and bury her bones. What was their amazement when at last they found the dead tree with the chain still around it but no sign of Psyche's remains. Swept with deep emotion, Orual looked this way and that, and as she and Bardia searched they came upon a ruby from the strap of one of Psyche's sandals. But this ruby lay in a direction where no one in Glome had ever dared to go, believing that beyond the tree lay the dreaded country of the gods.

Determined at whatever hazard to go forward, they moved cautiously and soon came to the brow of a steep slope. As they stood there the sun, which had been hidden before, shone warmly and revealed to them an exquisitely green and luxuriant valley with beautiful trees, wild gorse and vines and clear streams of water. As they descended, the bitter cold they had felt earlier on the mountain now disappeared and the air grew milder moment by moment. Bardia whispered to Orual that they were probably entering the secret valley of the god.

And here Orual and Bardia received the greatest shock of their lives. Just across a deep but narrow stream of water they saw Psyche herself. With mingled rapture and tears Psyche greeted them. She was so much more glorious than ever before that Bardia warned Orual her sister might now be a goddess. Soon Psyche was helping Orual across the stream and telling her how much she had longed for her.

Now Psyche told Orual a story of events quite literally out of the world, of how, after all the people had left the mountain, she could not escape the chains that bound her; how she had prayed and was thirsty without hope of water; how she had feared she might be eaten by some animal. But then, said Psyche to her sister, came wonderful relief, first a little breeze and then the smell of rain and then a great rain and with it such a wind that without her chains she would have blown away. And then—and then came Westwind himself and pulled her with his strong, loving arms right out of her chains and carried her away to his beautiful palace where she was bathed and dressed in splendid clothing and fed by unseen hands. And finally she told Orual how she now had a devoted husband who came to her each night and who laid but one small condition upon her—she was not to see his face.

Now Orual, though she saw Psyche before her bright-faced as a goddess, simply could not believe what she had heard, and concluded that she must carry Psyche away and properly mother her and restore her to her senses. Following an unhappy struggle the unsuccessful Orual returned reluctantly to Glome, puzzling all the way over her experience. After a time Orual, having gained no satisfaction either from Bardia or the Fox, determined at all costs to rescue her sister from the outlaw or whatever monster had taken advantage of her. So again Orual went up and over the Grey Mountain, this time with a dagger. When Psyche steadfastly chose her husband over her sister, Orual drew the dagger and, plunging it down through her own arm, threatened to kill both herself and Psyche unless she agreed to take a lamp and discover who her husband really was. Seeing the blood flow from Orual's arm poor Psyche was appalled enough to agree to Orual's command, though reluctantly.

Now Orual recrossed the stream overwhelmed with pain from her wound and with a greater agony of doubt over what she had done to Psyche. As darkness came on, Orual anxiously watched Psyche's palace. Sure enough, she saw Psyche's lamp light up and she imagined Psyche's discovery of some vile being who pretended to be her loving husband and Psyche hurrying out into the protecting arms of Orual and happiness for both of them. But instead of a vindication of her fears and a happy return to Glome, Orual beheld a great flash of lightning. A torrent of rain fell and swiftly the river rose. Above the roar she heard with anguish the sound of Psyche's weeping as she disappeared into the stormy distance. Then came another great flash of light directly over Orual and she saw in its center a god looking at her with measureless rejection. After a long silence the passionless but kind voice told her that because of her, Psyche must now go into exile and suffering.

Now Orual herself began a lifetime of suffering. Her father, the king, died and Orual became queen of Glome. She was a good queen and ruled well. But, desperately though she struggled, she could not erase the past events from her memory, especially that voice in the storm. She kept trying, but unsuccessfully, to puzzle out what had occurred. Eventually she decided to sit down and write her case against the gods.

She began by saying that the god of the Grey Mountain, the very one Psyche had always longed for, hated her. She told how with the birth of Psyche came the happiest season of her life, days and years when she and Psyche and the Fox were overflowing with joy together. She wrote down her account of the unspeakable terror of Psyche's being carried sacrifically to the mountain. The gods, she accused, were altogether bad, to bring such events to pass. Or were they? Did not the rain come in great abundance and the birds return and crops grow after Psyche was chained to the tree? A hundred times she recalled the shock of finding

Psyche radiantly alive in the green valley and her astonishing account of Westwind, her husband, and the shining palace in which she claimed to live. And Orual told how instead of the beautiful clothes Psyche claimed to wear she saw only rags; instead of the delicious food and wine she saw only wild berries and water.

But oh, there was that early experience when Orual, having left Psyche on the other side of the stream, at twilight had gone down to scoop up a drink and there on her knees looked up and saw—yes, momentarily she saw Psyche's palace, vast and glorious. But neither this nor the face of the benign but terrible god in the storm was able to satisfy Orual. Why, she kept asking in her complaint about the gods, why are they so secretive? Why do they come and go? Why can they not state plainly what they want? Thus she reviewed her case continually and remained torn and miserable.

In the meantime she endeavored to forget the sad circumstances she had managed to create and to kill the real Orual in herself through attention to her queenly duties. Bardia had taught her how to use a sword and Orual volunteered to settle differences between Glome and an enemy country by means of a personal duel with that land's champion. Despite the veil over her face, a veil she had resolved to wear always, she killed her opponent and made herself the pride of her people.

The years passed and she and Bardia and her army won other battles. Yet despite all efforts Psyche was always in Orual's memory. Where was she now? Sold into slavery? Dead? Destitute and repentant, a wanderer of the earth? Orual's antidote for such thoughts was to attend more and more to the needs of the people of Glome. As queen she was forced, on occasion, to appear ceremonially in the house of Ungit. She liked this task better after the old priest had died and the new priest had brought in a clean, Greek-fashioned goddess to replace the bloody Ungit. The

Fox grew old and finally died and Orual gave him a great funeral and buried him on the beloved spot where, in those long past joyful summers, he had taught her and Psyche his Greek philosophy.

But Orual continued writing her charges against the gods. Had they not brutally taken Psyche, her greatest love, and given her nothing in return? Had they not brought about those meetings with Psyche in the green valley while concealing from her the real truth? Was Psyche really the bride of a god? Why would they not give her some sign? And why had they left her the burden of deciding whether Psyche should live with her husband or go out as a sad sojourner? Why do the gods not go away and leave us to ourselves? Or else openly come and explain things and tell us plainly of themselves? Why hints and whispers? Why must the holy places be dim and dark always? Orual finally felt so sure of herself that she dared the gods to answer her, whatever curse it might involve. She concluded her charge against them by accusing them of being silent simply because they had no answer.

And this might have been Orual's final word had not the very act of writing down her case against the gods begun to stir deep inside her thoughts and passions which she had long since forgotten and which now arose more convincingly than she had ever dreamed. What she found was that the gods had used her very own pen to do their surgery in her heart. New understandings poured like stinging hailstones into poor Orual, yet, as she was about to discover, they were golden hailstones.

Among the first events was the death of Bardia, who was both the queen's most valuable adviser and the man she had for long years, without one overt word, ardently loved. Visiting Ansit, Bardia's widow, she was accused of destroying Bardia prematurely by overworking him. Though Orual went home very angry, she knew Ansit to be right. Loving to be with Bardia, and jealous of Ansit, she had heaped on him needless tasks to keep him near her at the palace.

Thus Orual began digging into all her motives and soon she was left disconsolate. But she was wrong in thinking the gods had nothing more to say to her. She now began to have a series of dreams and visions. In the first she saw herself as another Ungit like a spider gorged with lives of people, or like one of the birds sacrificed to the bloody Ungit, or like a temple prostitute grown old and decrepit. Horrified, she took down her old sword to slay herself but found she was too feeble to wield it. Then she went out to the Shennit, ready to drown herself but there a voice commanded her not to do it. She knew at once that this was a god's voice, and she said, "Lord, I am Ungit."

And now visions came to Orual in which she and her sister were forced to perform similar tasks. The first was to get some golden fleece from the rams of the gods who were large as horses, so Orual stole up on them but with one great joyful rush they knocked her down flat. Next she saw another (it was Psyche) gather glorious golden fleece from thorns where it had caught. A second task was to sort out a great pile of seeds of different kinds. She could not even begin, but she saw that for Psyche many ants came and quickly sorted out the seeds into piles. A third vision involved her and her sister walking over burning sands carrying a bowl to the river Styx and filling it with water. She saw a great bird come and taking Psyche's bowl, fill it and return it to her. But Orual, holding her empty bowl, was picked up by an eagle and taken into a place of judgment before a vast host of the dead. There she was commanded to read her entire complaint against the gods.

High above the multitude silently listening to her, Orual looked at what she was carrying in her hands and found it not at all the book she had long been composing but instead a shabby little thing in a pinched and savage scribble. Refusing at first to read, she was forced to go on, and what she read was not the well-rounded and unanswerable case she had supposed she was writing but rather the story of the real Orual behind the veil. She read how she had wanted to be "her own" and claim Psyche also as hers only. Even if the gods wanted Psyche's happiness, Psyche was not the gods' but hers. Let Psyche be hers even if she were damned. Concluding, Orual raved, "She was mine, mine, mine."

"Enough," came the command. Poor Orual found she had been reading her scribbled yet true story over and over and in a voice not her own. After a long silence before the multitude, the judge asked, "Are you answered?" and Orual found herself saying "Yes." She saw that her lifelong complaint had been only a venomous snarl pouring out of her all those years. She understood why the gods do not answer such complaints as hers and do not show themselves openly. It was because she had no face, only an incoherent babble that she foolishly thought she meant.

One of those who heard Orual's case was the Fox, now himself in this place of true reality, aware of what he now knew to be his own lifetime babble. He abjectly confessed that the philosophy he had taught Psyche and Orual though crystal clear was empty of fundamental content. Suddenly Orual remembered that she had dared the gods to answer her and she asked the Fox what her fate would be. He replied, "You will not get justice." When Orual, surprised, asked if the gods are not just, the Fox replied, "Oh, no. What would become of us if they were?"

And now came a last great set of revelations to Orual, the final one a vision in which Orual watched Psyche go down into the earth to acquire a casket of beauty from Death herself and bring it back to Orual. As Psyche went down and down Orual saw the people of Glome, then the Fox, and finally the trembling queen herself all trying desperately to stop her, that is, to shield her from death, really to keep her safe for themselves. But Psyche now paid attention to none of them and went deeper and deeper until she was out of sight. Then in the vision, the glorious Psyche returned from Death bringing the casket and handing it over to Orual.

At last, in the vision, Orual and Psyche were together again just as they used to be—but no, for now Orual had become another Psyche. "Did I not tell you," said Psyche, "that we should meet again at my house?" The beatitude of joy Orual felt seemed unsurpassable. But something greater was coming. Orual's old terrors now turned to an overpowering sweetness. Westwind was again coming, dreadful and beautiful beyond words. The beauty of the place was made far more beautiful by his coming. And as he came to them, Orual and Psyche stood together at the shining pool in the garden and there was not an Orual and a Psyche but only two Psyches, for Orual, after her long and disastrous journey, had now received eyes to see as Psyche saw in those days of her childhood when she longed for the god of the Grey Mountain.

Now the visions ceased and the aged but real Orual found herself in the garden of her own palace, her bitter complaint in her hands. Knowing that death was near, she wrote down with shaking hands her last words. Though she had once told the gods they had no answer, "I know now, Lord," she confessed, "why you utter no answer. You are yourself the answer."

∽

The reader of *Till We Have Faces* should first read Apuleius' account in the *Note* at the end of the book. Lewis says that the first time he read the ancient myth of Cupid and Psyche he felt some latent human value beyond the mere tale. What he does in this novel is to overlay the Apuleius story with Christian implications.

1. In Lewis's account two sisters find themselves presented with widely differing and momentous choices. They may choose the philosophy of Lysias the Fox, their much loved Greek mentor, who holds that reason and the laws of

nature are adequate to explain all things, or nearly so. Since life and death are "according to nature," we should stoically accept circumstances and events as they come to us.

Or the sisters may choose the way of Ungit, the fertility goddess of the people of Glome, who make sacrifices to her of pigeons and sometimes humans and believe that thereby their prayers are answered. It is a primitive blood-religion all but opposite to that of the Fox.

Or Psyche and Orual may choose the one true God.

2. The story from first to last is addressed to the "Greeks," by which Lewis means people in any period of history who hold to the Fox's philosophy. He felt our own century particularly needed to examine its misplaced faith in rationalism and scientism. One interested in this book may well ask himself whether in his whole life he has ever ascribed occurrences to other than rational cause and effect according to the laws of nature.

3. Actually the Fox found it impossible to practice his philosophy consistently. One recalls that St. Paul reminded the Greeks of his time how their own poets had said that all men live and move and have their being in God (Acts 17:28). Like all of us, the Fox was called by "the true Light" which illuminates every man coming into the world (John 1:9). Later the Fox did indeed confess that though his philosophy was as clear as water it was also as thin.

4. The people of Glome believed explicitly in blood sacrifices to their goddess and practiced their convictions thoroughly. Ungit represents one of the innumerable ways in which pagan peoples worshiped their gods—some of their practices utterly depraved, such as temple prostitution, and some symbolic of good, such as belief that blood is efficacious. Like many others, Lewis believed that the polluted streams of paganism flowed in the direction of the pure river of the blood of Jesus Christ, as he explains in his essay entitled "Myth Became Fact." The Old Testament

is replete with instances of corrupted worship and the steady command to return to the true God.

Which was best—the Fox's conventional nod to gods he did not really believe in or the life-and-death centrality of blood among the pagans of Glome? Is man, as the Fox basically believed, the measure of all things, even of God, or does he need, for his soul's health, to acknowledge his proper place in the order of the universe? Minimally we can say of Glome that it knew, as the Fox did not, that knees are for bowing to something greater than man and thus experienced the reality of a larger world than his. Glome's god is too great for words, says the old priest (1, V) who is perfectly willing to die for Ungit, an act that, in spite of Orual's fear and disgust for the temple of Ungit, stirs her admiration.

Lewis clearly favors the bloody Ungit over the Greek-style temple in the woods belonging "to one of those small peaceful gods who are content with flowers and fruit for sacrifices" (1, XXI). Perhaps comparison can be made with the differing sacrifices made by Cain and Abel in the early history of the human race (Genesis 4:3-5).

5. In many ways Psyche and Abraham are similar. Abraham's people in Ur worshiped a moon-goddess. We are not told in either case precisely why they, rather than others in their tribe, were clearly and surely separated from paganism to "a better sacrifice." Psyche longed with purity of heart from her girlhood for that better way, even while surrounded by Ungit worshipers. It is interesting that never in this story does she mention Ungit directly. Indeed, some portions of the great faith chapters (11 and 12) of Hebrews seem applicable to Psyche. She was, like Abraham, "looking forward to the city with solid foundations of which God himself is builder." Her eyes wre fixed on the "true homeland . . . a better country." We are told that the people of Glome had never been over the mountain which, for Psyche, was always the center of her heart's attention.

Like other people of faith, she was "exposed to the test of public mockery" and tempted by Orual "by specious promises of release." She also, like the ancient people of faith, "quietly produced the fruit of real goodness."

6. Psyche's long dream of the glorious mountain kingdom was fulfilled in her by her new husband. St. Paul told the Corinthian church that he saw it "like a fresh, unspoiled girl" whom he was presenting as fiancée to her "true husband, Christ himself" (II Corinthians 11:2, *Phillips*) The *New International Version* translates Isaiah 54:5 as:

> For your Maker is your husband—
> The Lord Almighty is his name.

Psyche may be seen as symbol of all Christians, i.e., people joined to Christ, whom as yet they have not seen, in a life-long loving relationship. St. Peter tells the Christians scattered in Asia Minor, "At present you trust Him without being able to see him, and even now He brings you joy that words cannot express." (I Peter 1:8, *Phillips*) Jesus told Thomas, who had demanded to put his hand into the wound in Christ's side, "Blessed are those that have not seen, and yet have believed." (John 20:29) Psyche regards even her husband's forbidding as a part of his love for her. The Green Lady in *Perelandra* willingly accepted Maleldil's command about the Fixed Land. So we may note Orual as another Un-man of sorts, one who in this instance actually coerces Psyche into disobedience.

7. Surprisingly, Lewis says that Psyche is not a Christ figure but rather is, as any Christian should be, "like Christ." (*Letters of C. S. Lewis*, p. 274) Thus he suggests that the purity, the longing for Christ, the giving of oneself in loving kindness and even the willingness to die for Christ, should be quite normal characteristics of the Christian.

8. What a fine person Queen Orual actually is, apart from her lack of genuine spiritual insight! She is clear-thinking, a hater of her father's rages and arbitrary decisions, an excellent ruler and a lover of justice. Though she is deeply

in love with Bardia, she never betrays it and treats him always with respect. She is not an atheist though she believes the gods to be evil and malignant. (As a boy Lewis once told his friend Arthur Greeves that God's strategy in bringing man to his senses is "cruelty after cruelty without any escape.")

Orual's real trouble is one that Lewis regards as central to humanity, that is, selfishness. Hers is particularly destructive because it masquerades as love for her sister. So Orual resents Psyche's longing for the Grey Mountain and hates Psyche's husband thoroughly enough to destroy her sister rather than allow their union to continue. Lewis explains the sad jealousy of relatives who are often shocked when one member of the family becomes a Christian or perhaps a Christian family who try to dissuade one member from becoming a foreign missionary, unwilling to face such a loss (*Letters, cf. C. S. Lewis*, p. 274). Orual longed to take away Psyche's liberty and mold her into her own image. Some people feel that becoming a Christian means surrendering oneself to a demanding and inscrutable master. But Lewis believed, very scripturally, that there is no true freedom other than the freedom given by Jesus Christ (John 8:36, Romans 8:2).

9. One must note that Orual as much as Psyche was called out of her paganism to the true God. From the very first, Psyche was open to the heavenly calling, while in Orual's experience more than forty years, most of them inwardly bitter ones, were required to reach the same end. One reason was that Orual had absorbed very much more of the Fox's philosophy than had Psyche.

10. Very much is said in this story about faces, the most significant being the veiled face, actual and symbolical, of Orual. By having a face Lewis means a willingness to be honest with the truths of the whole universe, not some selected ones that suit one's prejudices or a given climate of opinion. When she finally faced her judges, Orual, now

an old crone of a woman, had her rags snatched off her, her nakedness being the symbol that at last she was becoming honest. She was "getting a face." The Bible has much to say about faces and veils. One well-known passage is II Corinthians 3:12-15 where Moses veils his face to hide the fact that God's glory is fading from it, the Israelites' minds have been veiled to prevent their clear understanding but, by contrast we, with "unveiled faces," reflect the glory of God as we are changed into his likeness. The analogies with Lewis's thinking are clear.

11. It is important to notice that this story is divided clearly into two parts, the first being Orual's case against the gods and the second her changed views following the series of dreams and visions which revealed to her the real though hidden truth. She saw, for instance, the heavenly help given Psyche in sorting the seeds, gathering the golden fleece and acquiring the bowl of water and by contrast her own futile, human struggles to attain the same ends.

12. Most of all, Orual discovered what a pitiful case was hers when, finally, she was forced to stand before her judges and present it. (It may be the very case we or our neighbors are making at this moment, often a case that, unlike Orual's, is tenaciously clutched until death.) Standing naked before the great throng, Orual found her case no more than "a vile scribble" and far shorter than she had ever imagined, as well as being repetitive. Most interesting of all, she found it was not actually in her own handwriting. Her hatred of the gods and her determination to have Psyche as her very own had corrupted her ability to think straight and led to the life long veiling of her face. But she was better than her case, thanks to the Light which had never failed, even in her hatred of divine things, to light and enlighten her. Like St. Paul on the road to Damascus, she finally could admit "Lord, I am Ungit."

Orual found that the very utterance of her case against the gods was also the answer; that God never rejects one who in quietness and genuine honesty sits down to write, as Orual did, the case against Him, perhaps because God is looking for other Oruals to unveil.

13. As is customary in his stories, Lewis closes this one on a note of glory and joy. Orual had asked the Fox, now himself aware of his lifetime errors, if the gods would give her justice. His reply: Not so, for what would become of us if the gods were just? What she received instead of justice was an overwhelming mercy which replaced her lifelong ugliness with the same heavenly beauty which her sister, now herself repentant of her great sin against Christ, had once possessed and had reacquired.

14. One must always remember that Lewis is telling his story in myth and symbol, based on the old myth of Cupid and Psyche. Cupid we know as the god of love, and Psyche means, in Greek, soul, that is, the immaterial essence or spiritual principle resident in a human body. Psyche is lovingly rescued from captivity by Westwind, another character in Greek mythology, and here a symbol of Christ, whom the pagan people of Glome can see and fear only as the Shadowbrute. He becomes "husband" to one who from childhood had experienced a great longing (*Sehnsucht*) for him. Contrary to her sister Orual, who demands always to see, Psyche is willing to live by faith with her unseen Lord. Yet after her sin against him she is sent away broken hearted for a time, both as punishment for her own disobedience and also that God may speak through the event to Orual.

15. As in the redeemed John and Vertue at the close of *The Pilgrim's Regress* and in St. Anne's versus Belbury in *That Hideous Strength* (and indeed throughout all of Lewis's Christian works) we find a great difference in eyesight—or, better, spirit-sight—between the saved and the unsaved. How very blind poor Orual was, and that for most of a lifetime. How well Psyche saw, even from early childhood. How clearly Lucy Pevensie saw always, and how blind was

her sister Susan, even in the very presence of Aslan. How blind were all but one of the passengers on the bus from hell to heaven. How eternally clear sighted was the Green Lady and how myopic Weston. How often blind are the so-called great in any age and how seeing the humble and quiet of spirit. Lewis's insight into this difference between sight and blindness is no less explicit than that presented in the Bible itself.